D1738332

MOODS AND TRUTHS

MOODS AND TRUTHS

By

FULTON J. SHEEN

KENNIKAT PRESS
Port Washington, N. Y./London

Nihil Obstat: ARTHUR J. SCANLAN, S.T.D., *Censor Librorum*

Imprimatur: ✠ PATRICK CARDINAL HAYES, *Archbishop, New York*

New York, March 1, 1932

DEDICATED TO THE

Cherished Virgin Mary, Mother of Jesus,
Holy Gateway through which God came to men,
In prayerful supplication and petition that
Loving souls seeking Love may find thee: the
Door through which men pass back again to God.

PREFACE

This work, "Moods and Truths," is a continuation of the previously published "Old Errors and New Labels," and is concerned principally with religious thought as the latter was concerned with philosophical thought. Its title is derived from a comparison of the *moods* which dominate modern thinking, and the *truths* which inspire ultra-modern thinking. Its purpose is not critical, for in no instance is a mood subjected to criticism without a constructive doctrine being set up in its place; rather it seeks to orientate minds which have grown weary with fads and fancies that suit the times (which is all they do suit) and to direct them to those eternal and abiding truths which must ever remain the foundations of sound thinking because they are not man-made, but God-made.

The author wishes to acknowledge his profound thanks to Arthur Deering, Ph.D., Professor of English at the Catholic University of

America, who has so kindly read the manu-
script and suggested corrections to make it
more readable, and to James Allen Nolan,
M.A., for characteristically kind assistance in
correcting the proofs.

The author will not feel that his work has
enjoyed any success, even though its reception
be great or its praise high, unless at least a
single soul who may have chanced to read it,
is lifted up to a better living of that life which
is Divine, a better understanding of that Truth
which is the Word, and a deeper love of that
Love which is the Spirit of God. In a world
that is constantly looking for new faiths, new
religions, and new creeds, there could be nothing more new or novel than to begin to practise
and live the Truths of Christianity.

THE AUTHOR

CONTENTS

MOODS AND TRUTHS

THE THRILL OF MONOTONY

THERE is nothing from which the modern mind is more anxious to escape than the depressing bogey of monotony. It hates the mere fact of repetition just as much as it loves the shock of the new. The hatred of monotony is the explanation for many of the distorted views of life and action. The modern man hates the monotony of the same wife, and to escape it seeks refuge in divorce, where, instead of having wives in teams, like the Orientals, he drives them now in the modern fashion of tandems. The modern mind dislikes exceedingly living according to the morality of the Ten Commandments and the Christian Law of Charity, and to escape its monotony develops new morals and prefaces to morals and, without any of the thunder and lightning of Sinai, writes for itself a new ten commandments. Finally, the modern mind dislikes the monotony of a life that is consecrated to a single purpose and a final end, and to escape it, often with his own hand, man shuffles off this mortal coil. This positive distaste for repetition so characteristic of our day alone explains the new, the constant demand for new thrills, new excitements, new psychologies, new religions, new morals, new gods, new everything to arouse the already jaded sensibilities and the soul weighted down with world ennui.

If one asks just why monotony is so distasteful to our age, one is met with this answer: Everything that is full of life loves change, for the characteristic of life is movement toward a new goal, and urges toward new pleasures. Being essentially directed to novelty, life can never rest in the tediousness of repetition.

This argument has never appealed to thinking men as thoroughly sound. I believe that just the contrary is true, and instead of saying that those who are full of life hate monotony, we should say that those who are full of life find a positive thrill in monotony. To prove this point one can appeal to those who are essentially full of life and who, therefore, enjoy the thrill of monotony: namely, a child, God, and His Incarnate Son—Our Blessed Saviour.

First of all, the child. If you place a child

4

upon your knees and bounce it up and down three or four times, the child, full of the passion of life, will cry out, "Do it again." If you tell the child a delightful fairy-story, the child will never say, "Oh, that is an old one. I heard Aunt Kate tell that last week." But he will say, "Tell me again." If you are very clever and can blow smoke through your eyes, or even through your ears, the child is never content with just the one trick of magic, but will say, "Do it again." You may build houses of cards, and then tear them down, and feel that you have exhausted your repertoire when you have done it once, but the child is not so easily depressed with repetition, and with joyous appeal will sing out, "Do it again." Simply because the child is full of life, he wants to see things unchanged, and to have them repeated over and over again; for to his brimming enthusiasm, there is inseparably linked the wondrous thrill of monotony. And what is true of the child is true of God, or perhaps better, what is true first of God is true of the child and God —both love repetition.

When on that first great day of creation, God saw the first rose unfold its red petaled chalice

5

in tribute to Him, He did not feel that it would be a dull, drab world if roses went on producing roses till the crack of doom, and He did not ask that a rose should be turned into a stone. When He saw the first lily floating on the surface of a stagnant pond as if to testify that purity may blossom even when the environment is foul, He did not feel that it would be a monotonous world if lilies went on reproducing lilies until Gabriel sounded his golden trumpet, and so He commanded that every tree and every plant should reproduce itself according to its kind, for repetition is the sign of glowing and throbbing life. When He heard the first shrill notes of the canary, He did not think that the world would be dull and tiresome if canaries went on reproducing canaries and their song even to our own sad days. He did not ask that a canary be changed into a buttercup.

Because God is full of life, He enjoys the thrill that comes with sameness, and so I can imagine Almighty God with something of the joy and exuberance that belongs to a child, saying every morning to the sun, "Do it again," and every evening saying to the moon and stars, "Do it again," and every springtime say-

6

ing to the daisies, "Do it again," and every winter saying to the snowflakes chiseled by some great heavenly smith, "Do it again," and every minute saying to the mountain streams, as great silver ribbons, "Do it again," and every time a child is born in the world, to the eternal confusion of Birth Control, pleading for a divine curtain call, and asking for a Divine *Encore* in order that the heart of a God might once more ring out in the heart of a babe.

It was only natural, then, that when God sent His Beloved Son on to this earth He should teach the lesson that God taught at creation, namely, the gospel of the thrill of monotony. There was ever a beautiful monotony in the story of His life: thirty years obeying—not one year; three years teaching—not one year; three hours redeeming—not one hour. And as He lived He taught, and all His garnered wisdom could be summed up in the words, "Do it again." There was the monotony of sacrifice —"If any man will come after Me, let him . . . take up his cross *daily* and follow Me"; the monotony of kindness—"To him that striketh thee on the one cheek, offer also the other"; the monotony of birth—"Nicodemus, unless a man be born again . . . he cannot enter into the Kingdom of God"; the monotony of mercy—"How many times should we forgive? I say not to thee till seven times, but till seventy times seven times"; the monotony of sacrificial thoughtfulness—"Do this for a commemoration of Me"; the monotony of prayer—And the third time He went back again into the garden; the monotony of miracles, for St. John tells us that if he recorded all the miracles Our Blessed Lord had worked, the world would not be large enough to contain the books thereof. There was only one time in His life that He ever cursed a thing, and that was the day He saw the barren fig-tree which was not producing its fruit in due season, and therefore was not enjoying the thrill of monotony.

But it may be asked: "Why is there a thrill in monotony?" There is necessarily bound to be a thrill in working toward any goal or fixed purpose, and therein is the final reason for the romance of repetition. There, too, is the line of division between genuine Christianity and modern paganism. The Christian finds a thrill

8

in repetition because he has a fixed goal; the modern pagan finds repetition monotonous because he has never decided for himself the purpose of living. Instead of passing the test, the modern mind changes the test; instead of working toward an ideal, it changes the ideal; instead of tending repetitiously toward a fixed point, the modern mind changes its point of view, and calls it progress. It is no wonder life is dull, when one has not decided on what the purpose of life is; it is no marvel that existence is drab, if one has never discussed the reason for existence. How dull, for example, golf would be if there were never a green; how monotonous a theater, if there were never a last curtain; how monotonous would be a sea voyage, if there were never a port; or a journey, if there were never a destination. How insipid poems would be if there were never a last line, and heaven only knows how tiresome sermons would be, if there were never a last word, and so it is with life. Since the modern mind has never decided the goal of life, nor the purpose of living, nor the reason of existing, but like a weathercock has changed with every wind of doctrine and suggestion, it is necessarily bound to find life dull, drab, and monotonous.

Contrast this goalless existence with the Christian point of view in which a man has an ultimate end and purpose in life. Do you think, for example, that Dubois, who labored for seven years to make the cast for the statue of Jeanne d'Arc, found his artistic life dull and monotonous? Each day's work, repetitious though it was, brought to him the thrill of seeing the goal of the finished masterpiece come closer and closer. Do you think that the musicians or the scholars who practise and study for days upon days find their work monotonous? To them each repeated moment is just a preparation or a step toward the goal of either a thrilling recital, or a great intellectual discourse. Once admit a purpose in life, and each and every act which tends toward that point, bears the unmistakable stamp of joyfulness and cheer. The Christian has his fixed goal, namely, to make his life more and more Christlike. His own nature is like a block of marble, and his will is the chisel. He looks out upon his model, Christ, and with the sharp points of

10

his mortifying chisel, cuts away from his nature great huge chunks of cold selfishness, and then by finer and more delicate touches makes the great model appear forthwith, until finally only the brush of a hand is needed to give it its polished finish. There is no man living who has this Christian ideal who believes that repeated acts of faith, hope and charity, prudence, justice, fortitude and love are tainted with what the modern mind would call monotony. Each new conquest of self is a new thrill, for each repeated act brings closer and closer that love we fall just short of in all love, eternal union with Our Lord and Saviour.

Sometimes, of course, it is not always easy to see just how much progress we are making toward our goal, but though we never see the progress, we never lose sight of the goal. Then we are very much like the tapestry workers, who work not from the front of the tapestry, but always from the rear, keeping ever before their eyes the model of the work to be achieved. They go on drawing thread after thread in a monotonous but thrilling way, never destined to see their completed work until the last thread has been drawn, and the tapestry is turned about to show them how well and how truly they have labored.

> My life is but a weaving
> Between my God and me.
> I may but choose the colors,
> He worketh skillfully.
>
> Full oft He chooses sorrow,
> And I, in foolish pride,
> Forget He sees the upper,
> And I, the underside.[1]

The Christian, therefore, is always bound to have a great advantage over the modern pagan, simply because he knows where he is going, whereas the modern pagan knows nothing. The pagan must always be the pessimist, for he must always feel that this life is too short to give a man a chance, and the Christian will always be the optimist, for he knows that this life is long enough to give a man a chance for eternity. That is why the Christian can be joyful. That is why the pagan is sad and depressed.

Picture a child with a ball, and suppose that he is told that it is the only ball he will ever

[1] John Bannister Tabb, "Collected Poems."

have to play with. The natural psychological reaction of the child will be to be fearful of playing too much with it, or bouncing it too often, or even pricking it full of pin holes, because he will never have another ball. But suppose that the child is told that perhaps next month, perhaps next week, perhaps even in five minutes, he will be given another ball, which will never wear out, which will always give joy, and with which he will never tire of playing. The natural reaction of the child will be to take the first ball a little less seriously, and to begin playing with it joyously and happily, not even caring if some one does prick it full of pin holes, because he is very soon going to have another ball which will endure eternally.

The child with one ball is the modern pagan who has only one ball in the sense that he has one sphere, one world, one life, one earth. He cannot enjoy the earth as much as he would like because he must always be fearful of the earth being taken away from him. He can never even tolerate that any suffering or pain should ever come to his little ball, the earth, for it is the only ball that he will ever have to play with.

13

The Christian, on the other hand, is the one who believes that some day, perhaps even to-morrow, he will have another ball, another world, another sphere, another life. And so he can begin to play with this earth, enjoy its monotony, and even be resigned to its pin-pricks, for he knows that very soon he is going to have the other ball, which is the other life that will never wear out nor become tiresome, because its life is the life of the Eternal God, the beginning and the end of all that is.

When, therefore, seized and suffused through and through with the Christian ideal of making Christ shine out in your life; and, when in the routine of Christian living, you have begun your morning with a prayer and asked the Father's blessing on all your goings and comings; and when you have broken your fast with the Eucharistic Lord at the altar, and knelt in adoration before the uplifted Host and the glowing chalice; and when you have sanctified the day by offering each deed in union with the Master, and sanctified each trial by linking it with the Cross, and repressed unkind words and unjust criticisms out of love for Him who prayed for His enemies on the

14

Cross; and when the day is done you again kneel in thanksgiving and in humble gratitude to the Father of Light; and when after having done this day after day, week after week, and year after year in a constant effort to make your life more Christ-like; and then you wonder just what other thing needs to be done to bring you just a step closer to the goal of everlasting peace and happiness—then remember the lesson of the thrill of monotony, and "Do it again."

THE WORLD'S GREATEST NEED

THERE is a famine abroad on the earth—a famine not of bread, for we have had too much of that and our luxury has made us forget God —a famine not of gold, for the glitter of so much of it has blinded us to the meaning of the twinkle of the stars—but a famine of a more serious kind: one which threatens nearly every country in the world—the famine of really great men. In other words, the world to-day is suffering from a terrible nemesis of mediocrity. We are dying of ordinariness; we are perishing from our pettiness. The world's greatest need is great men.

There is little in the lives of men that is heroic, little that is genuinely self-sacrificing, little that is high. In the field of politics there are but few who follow principles rather than public opinion. The great majority of our men in political life instead of leading the masses by noble directions, follow them into ignoble ways. The age is too timid for individuality, too

calculating for enthusiasm, too weak for hero-
ism, and what is true in the political order is
true in the religious.

Religion walks in silver slippers. Its modern
prophets cannot cut against the grain of long
prejudices. They are jealously favorable to
modern views whether they be true or not,
just because they are modern. Our prophets
avoid taking sides when truth is concerned,
for fear they make enemies. They spread their
sails to every wave of popularity and would not
dare to say a word against a dominant prejudice
or a triumphant error. They enjoy the beatitude
that Christ never promised, and they enjoy it
because they are weak. It is not our institutions
that are failing us to-day; it is our men. We
need great men!

This statement about our civilizations suffering from the nemesis of mediocrity may be
challenged by an appeal to the so-called great
men of our day, for example, men of great
wealth who have started with nothing and have
amassed fortunes; men who have succeeded in
great feats of engineering, of tunneling under
rivers like moles, or spanning continents on
wings of steel. This is a type of greatness, I

will admit, but it is a greatness which is external to the man himself. Greatness is not in muscles, in gold, nor in educational institutions, nor in anything that strikes the eye. It consists in something that requires almost a new sense to appreciate. Greatness is not something external to man himself, but rather it is something internal to himself. Greatness is a quality of the heart and mind and soul by which man conquers not so much the tides of the sea, as the tides of his passion. Greatness consists in a fine sense of justice, righteousness, and charity; and judged by this standard it is true that we are equipped like gods to rule over nature, but to rule over ourselves we are equipped like pygmies, and yet it is in this self-conquest that true greatness consists.

The world's greatest need, then, is some one who will understand that there is no greater conquest than victory over oneself; some one who will realize that real worth is achieved not so much by activity, as by silence; who will seek first the Kingdom of God and His justice, and put into actual practice the law that it is only by dying to the life of the body that we ever live to the life of the spirit; who will brave the taunts of a Good Friday to win the joy of an Easter Sunday; who will, like a lightning flash, burn away the bonds of feeble interest which tie down our energies to the world; who with a fearless voice, like John the Baptist, will arouse our enfeebled nature out of the sleek dream of unheroic repose; some one who will gain victories not by stepping down from the Cross and compromising with the world, but who will suffer in order to conquer the world. In a word, what we need are saints, for saints are the truly great men.

Just suppose that we could turn loose in America at this time twelve saints. Let us assume that none of them were university trained, but that all their knowledge came from prayer; that they were not rich men, but poor, like St. Francis of Assisi; that they had all their beauty in their souls and not on their faces, like St. Vincent de Paul; that none of them were practical as the world counts practicality, but all of them impractical in the sense that but one fourth of their waking time would be spent in activity, and the rest in prayer. Suppose that these men who had laid upon them an invisible consecration, who had the zeal of Christ burning in their hearts, tore away the accumulated cobweb of our sophistry, confounded our conventional morality with sincerity, let the stroke of their challenge ring on the broad shield of the world's hypocrisies, paid no respect to slogans, preached the lesson of justice on street corners, and repeated at each available moment that it is only by being conformed to the passion of Christ that we can ever be conformed to the glory of His risen body!

What would follow if these men went into the world? A roar of execration! They would please no one. Belonging to no party, all parties would oppose them. Rich men would deride them. Learned men would ignore them. Modern Pharisees would lay snares for them, and call them politically dangerous. They would be called fools, fanatics, devils, mad. People would say that they were actuated by mawkish sentimentality; that their zeal was just a pretense; that they were mystics; that only the ignorant would follow them. They would have more stones thrown at them than other men have flowers. But these twelve men, these great men, would effect a greater spirituality in America than all the combined humanitarian agen-

23

cies counting tens of thousands of members. They would elevate more hearts and souls to the love of God; they would purge out more wickedness in a day than reformed societies would do in a lifetime, simply because they were great with the greatness of Christ.

Now we cannot all become saints as these twelve men that I have pictured, but we can all become saints to a certain degree, and I am going to try to explain in simple psychological terms how saints are made. I assume without further ado that the grace of God is the one thing necessary, and that God will give that grace to those who do His will. I am concerned merely with the natural elements of sanctity, or the psychological steps which lead to the state of sainthood, and these are three: a sense of emptiness, a knowledge, and an exchange.

First of all, I say that they are made by an experience of the emptiness of the world, and its absolute incapacity to give peace and happiness to the human heart. Consult your own experience. When you were children you looked forward to Christmas Day, and in anticipation you imagined all the joys that would be yours with the possession of your toys, the sight of the lighted tree, and the unlimited taste of fruits and candies. When finally Christmas Day did come, and you had played with the toys (and it was not long until you were "played out") and had tasted the sweetmeats and blown out the last candle on the tree, you then crept into your bed and said in your own little heart of hearts, that somehow or other, it did not come up to your expectations. It did not, for nothing does. That experience of childhood has been repeated a thousand times since. Men look forward to the possession of power—they finally get it, and still they are unhappy. Men crave wealth—they have a hundred times more than they need, and still they want more, and their wanting it makes them unhappy. Even the loss of the least of it robs them of joy, as the plucking of a single hair from a head that is full of it, gives pain. Nothing ever comes up to our expectations.

Well, why is it? The reason is that in looking forward to the things of this world, we use our imagination, which, as a faculty of the soul is spiritual, and therefore capable of imagining infinite things. I can imagine, for example, a mountain of gold, but I have never seen one. I

25

can imagine a castle on the Hudson that has a thousand rooms, and each wall blazing with diamonds and emeralds, but I have never seen that castle, and perhaps never will.

Now the pleasure of the future, the joys which I hope to obtain, the power which I desire to wield, the wealth which I desire to possess—all of these as long as they are not actually in my possession, become endowed with the infinity which belongs to the imagination. They, in a certain sense, become spiritualized and idealized, and hence take on something of the blessedness and infinity of my imagination. But when finally these imaginations or expectations are realized, they are material, they are local, definite, concrete, finite, cribbed, confined. In the mind they were ideal, and hence almost unbounded; in reality, they are concrete, and therefore very limited. Hence there arises a tremendous disparity between the infinite imagination I had of these things, and the finite realization. When the things actually do come, they come with a sense of loss. We feel that in their becoming actual or real, they lost something of the beauty with which we had imaginatively endowed them. A sense of emptiness or void then comes over the soul. We feel that we have been cheated out of something, for the realization compared to our imagination is like trying to fill a valley with a pebble; a terrible sense of emptiness creeps over the soul, and this sense of void is really a call of God. In very simple terms, it means that we cannot expect happiness here below. It also means we are made for an infinite happiness, otherwise we never could have imagined it. And it further means that we can never obtain it here below, for otherwise we would never have this terrible feeling of loss, and disappointment, and emptiness.

Two escapes are possible from this feeling of emptiness and dissatisfaction of the world, or better still, from the voice of God. One is to drown the call of God by seeking new pleasures, new stimuli, new excitements. Some souls use the remedy and go on chasing butterflies and golden pots at the end of the rainbow. They throw themselves into pleasures that satisfy a very small part of themselves, but never their whole being. Others let loose the reins of duty upon the flanks of the steeds of passion, and gallop down the avenues of pleasures, al ways being made more hungry by that which satisfies, until at last despair drives them to suicide and double death.

Saintly souls, on the other hand, when they feel this sense of uneasiness in their souls, conclude that happiness is not to be found on this earth; that they were made for God, and that their only unhappiness comes from a failure to tend toward Him. At this point begins the second stage in the development of great men, namely, a knowledge (and by knowledge I mean an understanding) of our Lord and Saviour. Let me here again appeal to your personal experience. You may have heard a great deal about a certain person, about his mannerisms, about his severity, about his rigorous life. You only know *about* him, but you do not *know* him. With this meager knowledge you frankly avow that you do not care for him. After spending five minutes in his company, your whole feeling has completely changed. Knowledge changed your whole outlook on him, and converted hate into the beginning of love. In much the same way that the prejudice of Nathaniel against our Blessed Lord was changed by just two sentences from our Lord's

28

lips, sentences which swept away prejudice, so it is with the soul of a great man before our Lord. At a distance Our Lord seems to be a harsh Master bearing a crown of thorns upon His head and a cross upon His shoulders. We fear lest having Him we must have naught else beside. Then one day we meet Our Lord, perhaps in sorrow or in pain, and we pass five minutes with Him, and our whole outlook on Him completely changes. We see now that the crown of thorns is the prelude to the halo of light and the cross the prelude to the empty tomb, and then we hear Him sweetly say:

All which I took from thee, I did but take,
    Not for thy harm
But that thou mightest seek it in My arm:
All which thy child's mistake
Fancies as lost. I have stored for thee at home;
    Rise clasp my hand and come. . . .
For whom will thou find to love
        Ignoble thee, save Me, save only Me.[1]

At this point begins the third stage of sainthood, namely, exchange. There is a wrong im-

[1] Francis Thompson, "The Hound of Heaven."

29

pression in the world to the effect that following Our Lord means giving up the world, abandoning friends, surrendering wealth, and losing all that life holds dear. If we fear that in having Him we must have naught else besides, we have not begun to understand Christ.

Such is not really the case. Sanctity is not a question of relinquishing or abandoning or giving up something for Christ; it is a question of exchange. Our Lord never said it was wrong to love the world; He said only that it was a loss, for "what shall a man give in exchange for his soul"? Exchange is founded on the fact that there are two classes of goods. First, things that we can get along without; secondly, things we cannot get along without. I can very well get along without a dime, but I cannot get along without the bread which it will buy, and so, I exchange one for the other. So, too, in the spiritual world. I soon learn that there are many things that I can get along without, and as I grow in acquaintance with Christ, I find that I can get along without sin, but I cannot get along without His peace of conscience, and so I exchange one for the other. Later on, as I get to know Him better, I find

30

that I can get along without an innocent pleasure, but I cannot get along without the pleasure of daily communion with Him, and so I exchange the one for the other. I find, by a still deeper acquaintance, that I can get along without the world's goods, but not without the wealth of Christ's grace, and so, I exchange one for the other, and that is the vow of poverty. I find that I can get along very well without the pleasures of the flesh, but I cannot get along without the pleasures of Christ's spirit, and I exchange the one for the other, and that is the vow of chastity. I find that I can get along very well without my own will, but I cannot get along without His, and so I exchange the one for the other, and that is the vow of obedience. Thus the saint goes on exchanging one thing for another. And thus it is that in making himself poor, he became rich, and in making himself a slave, he became free. The gravitation of the earth grows weaker, and the gravitation of the stars grows stronger, until finally, when there is nothing left to exchange, like Paul he cries out: "For me to die is gain," for by that last exchange his gain is Christ in everlasting life.

Sanctity, then, is not giving up the world. It is exchanging the world. It is a continuation of that sublime transaction of the Incarnation in which Christ said to man: "You give Me your humanity, I will give you My Divinity. You give Me your time, I will give you My eternity. You give Me your bonds, I will give you My omnipotence. You give Me your slavery, I will give you My freedom. You give Me your death, I will give you My life. You give Me your nothingness, I will give you My all." And the consoling thought throughout this whole transforming process is that it does not require much time to make us saints; it requires only much love.

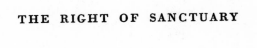

THE RIGHT OF SANCTUARY

THE RIGHT OF SANCTUARY

IN THESE days it is almost impossible to call our souls our own, for the psychoanalytic mood has seized us like a pestilential fever. Every sin and failure of a soul, every crime and secret passion of a heart, every unholy falling from a holy purpose is broadcast to a world which believes it finds a justification of its own wrongs in hearing the wrongs of others. Even the most cursory review of the present day, reveals a piquant desire on the part of the press, biographers, novelists, and even historians to analyze feelings, relate inner experiences, minutely trace sentiments, not so much because these sentiments are laudable and worthy of imitation, but because they are racy and therefore full of excitement. Great men and women of the past have their lives reviewed, not so much for praise as for dissection. Even well-known figures of the present, seized by this psychoanalytic mood for revealing passions, and disclosing impulses, write not so

35

much of what is best in their character, but what is most hidden in it, and particularly those feelings and urges of the lower nature which a generation ago would not have been mentioned in a whisper. Then, too, there is in our country, published for tabloid minds, a certain kind of newspaper which never mentions the hidden lives of the innocent, nor the sacrificing outpourings of mothers, nor the devotion to common duties, but is eloquent about divorce, murders, broken vows, infidelities, and the thousand and one other sins destined to excite our jaded sensibilities, to quicken our lust for sensation, and if possible to thrill, by appealing not so much to virtue as to vice. Judgment Day seems to be anticipated, for in the valley of the new Jehosophat there is nothing hidden; all is revealed. The great woe of our wounded world is the woe of violated sanctuaries and by that I mean the sanctuaries of human souls.

In the face of this condition the world needs an institution something like that which flourished in the Middle Ages—namely, the Right of Sanctuary, which was based upon the inviolability attached to sacred things. A fugitive guilty of a felony was considered immune from prosecution by law, provided he entered the sanctuary of a church. The principle behind this right, was that any criminal who entered into the sanctuary had equivalently cast his lot with God, and, therefore, was immune from the searchings of men. In the great Cathedral of Durham in England there is still to be seen a large ring on the door, the holding of which gave to the criminal the right of sanctuary and immunity from inquisitiveness, at least for a period of thirty days.

The world to-day needs just some such right of sanctuary, wherein poor tired hearts might be free from the curious inquisitiveness of the press; it needs some haven wherein we might be alone with ourselves and our God, free from the publication of our sins to the world; some place of shelter from the curious eyes of those who, rather than bind up our wounds, delight in our outpourings; some solitary harbor where we might escape those who, though they ask us to reveal, never stop to heal; some sanctuary where our sins would not be told to the world, nor allowed to fester unseen within our heart; some sanctuary from which we

37

could pour out our souls to the God of love for the purposes of peace and pardon. And the world has such a sanctuary which respects the inviolability of the human person, a sanctuary wherein a soul may cast its lot, not upon inquiring men, but upon a forgiving God, and that is the Sacrament of Penance, or Confession.

What does confession demand? It demands two things; a confessor and a penitent. Only God could find both. First of all then, confession demands a confessor: a man who will look kindly on the denying Peters, speak words of forgiveness to penitent Magdalenes, breathe words of comradeship to betraying Judases; a man who will utter a cry of forgiveness as if from a cross to all those who would malign him or his office; a man with intensity of love for his work and with universality of love for his penitents; a man endowed with the wisdom that comes with training, one in whom the Church has laid the wisdom garnered from twenty centuries experience with souls; a man signed with the sign and sealed with the seal of Christ, and therefore, one who can love without loving; a man with discretion, that is, with

38

a mind strange to curiosity, vanity, and fear; and, finally, a man with a heart like an immense well into which sins like stones may be dropped, but a well so deep that no sound comes back from those depths to an ear which might be bent to hear.

But immediately it is said: "Why should I confess my sins to a man, for the priest is but a man? Why should I not tell them directly to God? Why should a confessor stand between my God and me?"

Why should a confessor stand between my God and me? For the same reason that the human nature of Christ stands between His divinity and me. If we were angels, there might be a confession of spirit to spirit, but being made up as we are of body and soul, it is fitting that body or a human nature be the means by which we commune with God. When God came down to earth in the Incarnation, He did not come as a flash of lightning, or as an invisible spirit, but He came in the form and the habit of man, and through that human nature of His, He forgave sins, lifted up blinking eyes to the light of God's sunshine, and healed hearts wounded with disease and death. God came to

39

us by taking a human nature, and through it as an instrument, He communicated His divine forgiveness. Ascending into heaven, it was only natural that He continue His forgiveness in exactly the same way, namely, through the instrumentality of other human natures, or, confessors.

Is it asking too much that you confess your-self to some one who has been constituted a delegate of divine justice and divine mercy? Is it asking too much that God should send out ambassadors to deal with those who have broken off relations with Him? At the present time, diplomatic relations are broken off be-tween Russia and the United States. The United States, therefore, never deals through direct diplomatic channels with the Soviet Government. If she has any dealings with the Soviets, it is through a third party. Is it not just, therefore, that since man, by sin, has broken off diplomatic relations with God he should deal with God through the inter-mediary of His ambassadors? Why should we admit this to be just in one case, in the case of human government, and deny it to be just in the case of divine government? And, as a mat-

40

ter of fact, does not God deal with our fellow-men through ambassadors in other walks of life? The source of all law is God, and the presidents and kings and parliaments throughout the world, in the administration of law, are really acting in His name. God has even given to heads of government the power of taking away life. If, therefore, some men share God's justice by punishing, why should not others share God's mercy by forgiveness? It is the very order of life that we should have the doctor for our body, the teacher for our mind, the president for our government. Why, then, should we not have confessors for our souls?

But it is immediately objected: "Grant that God does intend that His mercy should come to us through confessors, just as His justice comes to us through governors, but why should I confess my sins to a man, even though he is divinely commissioned? Why should it not suffice for me to bury my head in my handkerchief and ask God forgiveness? Why should I be obliged to tell my sins to the confessor?

For this reason, certainly if for no other, namely, because Our Lord intended that it should be so when He instituted the Sacrament

41

of Penance in these words: "Whose soever sins ye forgive, they are forgiven unto them: whose soever sins ye retain, they are retained." If Our Lord had spoken only of forgiving sins, the necessity of confession might not have been so clear, but when He added the words about retaining, He implied the hearing of sins in no uncertain terms, for how could confessors know which sins to forgive and which to retain, unless they knew the sins, and how would they know the sins unless they had been told, and what is the telling but confession?

If all we had to do was to bury our head in our handkerchief and make a few grimaces of repentance, grimaces which cost us nothing, and obligate us to nothing, since they are made alone, and in which we remain the judge of our own accusation, the door would be open to all manner of fraud and self-deceit. God, knowing the human heart, understands there is such a great tendency in it to compromise, to excuse, to extenuate, to palliate, that no one can be the judge of his own case. Conscience is generally too elastic. It accommodates itself too easily to sophisms, and a false interpretation; it is too

42

inclined to justify itself and to compromise. Added to this is the false justification of society; its grandiloquent vocables, and its high scientific names, its displaced responsibility and its denial of moral guilt and sin—all of these falsify and film over the true state of a soul.

There is nothing that so elevates the moral dignity of man as the penetrating look of an outsider. For a man to pardon himself in an instant by a simple act would be to destroy in man the root of all expiation and reparation. His plea for pardon might be just a mere fantasy. It costs a man nothing to confess his sins to God, for God knows them already. But it costs him something to reveal them to some one like unto himself, and by the very act of confessing his sins to man, he has already done some expiation for them. It is a point of law that no criminal may judge his own case, just as no doctor may diagnose his own disease, and no student may act as his own professor. The whole process would be in contradiction to the nature of things. The criminal at the bar cannot take the seat of the judge and mete out his own sentence. If he did, it would be the end of law. In like manner, no sinner may be his own judge, for it would be the end of justice.

Confessing to man is not too difficult. Almighty God might have ordained that we should tell our faults to the universe, for it is only just that the universe should know what we really are, but Divine Mercy has ordained nothing of this kind. The sin confessed is not broadcast, but locked in the secret storehouse of God, and because the institution of confession is surrounded by an inviolable secrecy and thus freed from the ravages of publicity, the act of confession is not destined to discourage a sinner. Not even an outside witness is called in, as in the case of civil law. The criminal confesses and hence is his own witness against himself. One might almost say he is the very jury which condemns himself. Nowhere in the law courts of the world can such order and mercy be found.

Confession demands not only a confessor, but also a penitent, and here, too, the wisdom of God is supremely revealed. The penitent must be created by God as the confessor was created by God. Making a penitent means taking a man in his pride and the icy silence which envelopes the avenues of his soul, and saying to him: "You shall come and kneel at the feet of a man who, in his human estate, may be no better than you are, but who is nevertheless an ambassador of Christ, and to that man you shall reveal that which you hid from your friends and relatives, that which makes you blush when alone, that which you lock in the closet of your memory, and, as you confess these secrets on bended knees, you shall say to that man: 'Father, forgive me, for I have sinned.'"

Hard though it is, this narration of sins by a penitent answers a need of the human heart. How often history reveals that a guilty man pressed by conscience alone, and driven on by some mysterious influence, stronger even than the conservation of life, will make him refuse the impunity which silence promises and will force him to proclaim the very sin the avowal of which will bring the punishment he sought to avoid. In moments when man has feared neither witnesses nor tortures, he cries out: "Yes, it is I. I did it." There is something even in the most hardened criminal at times which

45

makes him give himself up to justice by an avowal of his guilt, in order that he might have peace of mind.

Just as a foreign substance, like a piece of glass which is taken into the body, is gradually thrown off by the body, and just as a poison taken into the stomach irritates it until the stomach finally throws it off, so too, the heart of man, irritated and weary by the poison of sin, seeks the catharsis of spirit by which it, too, may pour its wrong and the poison of its sins into the ear of a friend.

And even those who have no great crimes upon their souls, but are weighed down by a heart which seems not right with God, they crave for some confidant to whom they can unpack their hearts through words. In joy and in sorrow, every heart needs some one who will suspend his own preoccupations to listen to its own articulation, needs some one who will drop all his cares to take on the burden of its own. The most unfortunate mortals are those who shed their tears in silence and find no one to wipe those tears away. How many men and women there are in the world who, through sin, have felt themselves alone, cast off from

46

every one, who in their inmost heart have felt
the need of some sanctuary into which they
might retire for consolation and direction. Our
cities are full of souls who are constantly crying out, "What can I do?" and to these and the
millions who are craving for some one who will
understand and pardon, as Christ understood
and pardoned weak Peter and sensuous Magdalene, the confessional is the answer.

Furthermore, in defense of the penitent's
side of the case, does not experience reveal and
history tell us that an honest avowal of our
guilt has a certain reparative value? All humanity has recognized in a spontaneous confession the quality of expiation and the merit
of pardon. Only one sentiment dominates this
point—from the mother who interrogates her
child in an attempt to make the child openly
avow its faults by saying, "Tell me and I will
not punish you"; up to the honor systems in
our colleges under which young men are told
to be men enough to "stand up" and acknowledge their guilt; on finally to the judge who interrogates from his bench the criminal—and
that sentiment is one which tempers the punishment when a man pleads guilty.

Now, if a man himself accords pardon on the ground of repentance by humbly avowing his fault, why should not God do the same on similar conditions? That is precisely what Our Blessed Lord has done. He has taken the natural avowal which has an expiatory force and elevated it to the dignity of a sacrament. An avowal is human but He has divinized it. What is natural He has made supernatural. That which has always been the indispensable condition for granting pardon, namely, the open avowal of guilt, is the condition upon which Almighty God has granted His pardon in the sacrament of Mercy. And so with that infinite tenderness of Him, He told the story of the prodigal son who came back to his father, acknowledged his guilt, and was rewarded with the embrace and kiss of his father. Such is the joy of God on sinners returning, for "even so there shall be joy in heaven upon one sinner that doth penance, more than upon ninety-nine just who need not penance."

Let it not be said that men instituted the Sacrament of Penance, for no man would ever have given to it such a form of procedure. A man is not naturally so reverential, or so amiable in regard to another, that he would lay open his whole soul even to a stranger. Let no one say that a priest has invented this Sacrament of Mercy, for if he had, human as he is, he would have excluded himself from its humiliations. Yet, no priest, no bishop, no cardinal, not even the Holy Father himself is immune from its laws. Let those who say that the confessional was instituted by a priest sit in the stuffy confessional boxes of our churches for five or six hours on Saturdays and feast days, and eves of First Fridays, listening to the routine misgivings and failings of human nature, and he will immediately avow that there is no human pleasure in such work, and that the only reason any priest does such work, which is the most trying of all his labors, is because he knows and feels that he is carrying on the blessed ministrations of Our Lord and Saviour, Jesus Christ.

There have been statements made recently that the confessional can be supplanted by psychoanalysis. This, however, is not true. The confession cannot be supplanted by psychoanalysis. There is a twofold difference between psychoanalysis and confession: the first is in what is told, the second is the reason for telling it. Psychoanalysis is the communication of mind with mind; the confessional is the communication of conscience with conscience. In psychoanalysis there is merely a confession of ideas, and the confession of ideas costs nothing and never craves pardon. In fact, there may be boastfulness about the confession of ideas. There are half-baked intellectualists who would boast of being atheistic, or who would say, I am an unbeliever; I am an agnostic; I am a nihilist. It is very easy to hold ideas, even ideas that have terrible consequences, but confession is not the communication of ideas; it is the communication of wills, and that is what makes it difficult. The mind does not blush in confessing that it is an atheist, but the will does blush when it admits that it has done wrong, because the will is under the domain of conscience. Even without an act, the sinner will blush sometimes at his own degraded intention, though no one in the world knows about it but himself. And the real healing of wounded hearts and wounded souls is not by the confession of wrong ideas but by the confession of wrong intentions and sinful deeds, not by telling of ideas but by the confession of sins, and that is why psychoanalysis may always develop in the way of pride, while confession will always develop in the way of humility and pardon.

Confession is different from psychoanalysis not only in what is told, but also in the reason for telling it. The reason for telling things in psychoanalysis is to acquire mental ease; but the reason for telling sins in the confessional is to acquire pardon. Psychoanalysis is on the plane of medicine; man is treated in the same manner as an animal might be treated. But confession is on the plane of justice; man is treated as a sinner. Psychoanalysis tells things for the sake of sublimation, but not for the sake of purgation. It is not enough to diagnose a disease: it must be also cured, but there is no cure for a guilty conscience except pardon. The sinner must in some way be brought to Calvary and made to see the personal equation between himself and the sufferings of Christ, and this is done only in the confessional.

If the world had never enjoyed the sacrament of penance, and some one proposed instituting it, there would be a universal cry go

51

up from all men saying that "humanity is too proud," and hence, there will never be penitents. "Humanity is too indiscreet," and hence, there will never be confessors. But the fact, here I speak as a priest among priests, that the world comes to our feet, children of seven years and their elders of seventy, hearts of sixteen years, hearts of sixty years, that fact that there come the mother with her daughters, the father with his sons, the precious desires of youth with the chagrins of old age, the innocent souls who never lost baptismal grace and the great prodigals who lost it and found again the fountains of mercy, and the fact that all these tell us that which the ear of a spouse does not hear, nor the ear of a brother know, nor the ear of a friend suspect, proves and proclaims to the world that there are penitents because there are confessors, and there are confessors because there are penitents, and there are both because Jesus Christ is God.

There is no institution in the world so effectively working for social reform as the Church through the confessional, and this for the double reason that the confessional gets at the intention which inspires the act, and reforms

52

the group by reforming the individuals which make up the group. The Church in the confessional, after the manner of her Divine Founder, proceeds on the principle that if it is wrong to do a certain thing, it is wrong to think about that thing. She does not wait until the desire or the intention passes into act; rather she goes into the very confines of a conscience and lays her finger on the desire to sin and brands it as a sin even though the desire is never realized. Mindful of the words of Our Blessed Lord, she does not wait until a man actually and physically commits adultery, but she holds that any man commits adultery even if he lusteth after a woman in his own heart. She demands that the defaulting cashier confess his intention to steal money, even though he finds it impossible to steal it. She holds, as against modern morality, that it is too late to legislate when the act has been done; it is too late to pass a law when you have to call a policeman; it is too late really to heal when you have to establish fact-finding commissions. The facts of crime, drunkenness, and social evils are merely the putting into action of base thoughts, intentions, and desires; and the

53

Church in insisting that every illicit motive and every evil desire be confessed is getting at the hidden springs and roots of action, and in keeping them clean she keeps actions clean; by making man pure on the inside, she makes him pure on the outside; and by making him right with God, she makes him right with his fellow-man.

The Church in the confessional is, furthermore, the only institution in the world to-day which reforms society by reforming the individual. Modern social reform begins with the group and ends with the group. Modern morality talks about crime, which is a group problem; the Church in the confessional talks to the criminal, which is the individual problem. Modern morality talks in the abstract about the problem of drunkenness; the Church in the confessional talks in the concrete to the drunkard and asks him not to psychoanalyze his mental state for sublimation, but to reveal his moral state for purgation. And of these two methods, the confessional is the only really effective one, for just as the only way to make a family good and happy is to make each individual in the family happy, so, too, the only way to make society peaceful is to make each individual citizen peaceful, and this cannot be done except by making each conscience right with its God. Modern morality is in a tower shouting to rebellious soldiers below; the Church through her officers is mingling with the soldiers individually, bidding each one to submit to law which is, in the last analysis, the ordinance of God. Thus it is that by making individual adjustments, and by treating each conscience singly, and judging it not by the way it makes for worldly success, but by the way it is ordered to God, the confessional purifies each individual stream and river that runs into the great social ocean, and if that ocean to-day does not seem clean and bright, it is only because there are some streams that have not been made clean at their source by the distilling and refining pardon of God's great Sacrament of Mercy.

If, therefore, our government and our social reformers are really sincere about the betterment of society, they must begin to recognize the importance of intention and the importance of the individual; they must more and more see that we cannot allow citizens to think badly and expect them to act rightly, nor can we expect a commission to legislate morality for a nation without, in some way, seeing that each individual in the nation is himself moral and righteous with his God. We will not be made a moral nation by permitting our educators to tell us there is no such thing as sin, nor will we be made a righteous nation by permitting reformers to emphasize sin to the point of morbidity. There is only one way to have the fact of sin, and not to have the fact of its over-emphasis, which is morbidity, and that is through the confessional which tells a man that he is a sinner, but also tells him that he can, by God's pardon and grace, become a saint.

There is a fable about a man being locked in a little box, and when the box was opened it was found that he had the heart of a giant. That box is the confessional box, and the heart of the priest is the heart of a giant, and from the heart of that giant there come the consoling words of Christ—"Come to Me, all you that labor and are burdened . . . and find rest to your souls." And the penitents who hear those words then begin to understand the tremendous paradox of God's pardon: if we had never sinned we never could call Christ, "Saviour."

THE   DIVINE   SENSE   OF   HUMOR

A REMARK not to be taken too lightly is one to the effect that the modern world is taking itself too seriously. Whether there be only five senses or fifty-seven senses, one of the most precious of them all is the one the modern world is rapidly losing, namely, the sense of humor. There are many evidences to justify this statement that the world is losing its sense of humor. Note, first of all, the changed attitude toward laughter. It was not so long ago that laughter was as free as the air, and as spontaneous as a sneeze, being the natural product of human fellowship, and the joyous effervescence of friend meeting friend. Now it is put on a commercial basis, and the business of making people laugh has become one of the serious enterprises of our country; in fact, so serious has it become that we are now obliged to pay about two dollars for an evening of it in a theater.

Gold, too, is taken so seriously to-day that

some men pursue it as if it were the "be all and the end all here," as if shrouds had pockets, and coffins had coffers. If it is lost, some feel that life is no longer worth living. Another evidence is the seriousness with which the modern world embraces every new fad and fancy in the intellectual order, simply because it is new. The only real explanation for the craze over every new psychology, which lost its soul, then its consciousness, and now has lost its mind, or the only real explanation for the equally absurd theory that everything wrong in life is traceable to a sex libido, is that the modern world has lost its sense of humor. If these absurd theories about God being a creature of Space-Time, and religion being, as one philosopher put it, "a projection into the roaring loom of time of a unified complex of psychical values," were advanced fifty years ago, people would have laughed them out of existence. The only reason the modern world holds them is because it has lost its appreciation of what is funny; it has lost its sense of humor.

The problem of humor is best studied in relationship to this visible world of ours, and in order that we might more clearly grasp its history, we ask ourselves three questions: When did humor come into the world? When did the world lose its sense of humor? How did it regain it?

The Origin of the Divine Sense of Humor: There never was a brush touched to canvas, nor a chisel to marble, nor a dome thrown against the vault of heaven's blue, but that a great idea preceded it, for all art is the expression of the ideal through the real. The architect, for example, who conceived the Cathedral of Notre Dame, had an idea of that cathedral in his mind before a single stone of it was put upon stone. If he had lived to see his work completed, he would have seen in that stone tribute to the Blessed Mother, the realization, the consecration, or the petrifaction of his idea.

Now Creation is an art—the Divine Art of the Divine Artist. Everything that exists in this world, every stone, every diamond, every plant, every tree, every animal, every bird, every man, every child was made according to a Divine Idea existing in the Mind of God from all Eternity. God, too, had His "models" or "patterns" and these were the "archetypal

63

ideas" according to which all things were made. When, therefore, the Divine Fiat spoke to Nothingness, and planets and worlds tumbled from God's finger-tips, and the great procession of life moved on, everything which existed either in the most distant planet, or on our tiny earth, was a realization, or a materialization, or an incarnation of His ideas.

Almighty God willed that just as any great painting should make us think of the artist, and every great monument should remind us of the architect who designed it, so, too, everything in this world should, in some way, remind us of Him. In other words, God made the world with a *Divine Sense of Humor*.

But what has this to do with a Divine Sense of Humor? Do we not say that a person has a sense of humor if he can "see through things," and do we not say that a person lacks a sense of humor if he cannot "see through things"? But God made the world according to such a plan that we were constantly to be "seeing through things" to Him, the Power, the Wisdom, the Beauty, and the Source of all that is. In other words, the material was to be a revelation of the spiritual, the human the revelation

64

of the divine, the fleeting and the passing, the revelation of the Eternal. The universe, according to His original plan, was transparent, like a window pane, and according to that plan a mountain was not just a mountain; a mountain was the revelation of the power of God: a sunset was not just a sunset; a sunset was the revelation of the beauty of God: a snow flake was not just a snow flake; a snow flake was the revelation of the purity of God. Everything told us something about God, for by the visible things of the world is the power and wisdom of the Invisible God made manifest. According to this plan, every man was a poet, for a poet is one who is endowed with this sense of the invisible, the power of *seeing God through things,* and such is the essence of humor.

The Loss of the Sense of Humor: Such was God's Creation, or rather its great drama, perfect in detail, without flaw or blemish. But the drama, with each line exquisitely sketched by God, was given to man to act and to play, and man made a botch of the masterpiece. That one thing which destroyed man's plan in Creation, though not God's plan, was sin, and sin is seriousness. Sin is an act by which man re-

65

fuses to use creatures as stepping stones to God, or as a means to an end. Sin insists on using them as ends in themselves. As a man loses his sense of humor when he cannot see through a point, so, too, he loses his sense of humor in its entirety when he ceases to see things as revelations, or symbols, or reminders of God, and begins to regard them seriously as ends in themselves. The day sin came into the world, the world lost its transparency, and became opaque, like a curtain. A veil was drawn between the Artist and His artistry, between the Architect and the architectures, between the Creator and the creation. The sense of the invisible was lost. In his mental short-sightedness, man lost the power "to see God through things": then a mountain was just a mountain; a sunset was just a sunset; a snowflake was just a snowflake. Poetry passed out of the world, and prose came in—prose, a matter-of-fact-ness of style—and men settled down to that terrible seriousness in life which must always characterize those who cannot see beyond the veil.

Some men took matters so seriously that they hardened into materialists, while others took themselves so seriously that they congealed into atheists. And in all those sad days, when man sought gold for the sake of gold, there was nothing which so much set itself up as a badge of seriousness as the stone, silver, and brass images of gods that lined the streets of Rome and Athens. Each of these was an avowal of the confusion of paganism. The power to see God through things had been lost in the darkness wherein God was only a thing.

Rebirth of the Sense of Humor: This seriousness pervaded the world for full forty centuries. Then one night there rang out over the stillness of an evening breeze, the cry of the heart of a God in the voice of a child. Two classes of men heard the cry that night—shepherds and wise-men: the very simple, and the very learned; those who know they do not know anything, and those who know they do not know everything. They came to a cave, and to enter the cave they had to stoop: that was the stoop of humility. And there they found a Babe on straw whose eyes seemed to shine like two celestial suns. But they saw not only a Babe, for they had brought a new vision into the world. They saw *through* the Babe, or the

Divinity that was in Him: they looked on tiny hands that clutched only clumsily at the straw of the threshing floor, and yet through them they saw the hands of a God, hands which could raise up children of Abraham from the stones of the street; they looked at the tiny brow that had only just begun to tingle with human life, and through it they saw the mind of a God who might have spoken the secrets of every living heart that hour; they looked on tiny lips, and through them saw the lips which one day would pronounce a sentence of judgment on the living and the dead; they looked on tiny feet, and through them saw feet that trod the everlasting hills and stood firm under the weight of Divine Omnipotence. Those onlookers were really seeing more than a Babe in a crib. They were seeing God through a Babe: the Word had become Flesh: God was with us!

And when the Babe grew in grace and wisdom, He went into the public lanes and marketplaces, and began to teach a new doctrine to men—the doctrine of the Divine Sense of Humor. Everything He said, everything He did, could be summed up in these words: *Nothing in this world is to be taken seriously, nothing* —except the salvation of a soul. "What shall it profit a man, if he gain the whole world, and suffer the loss of his soul?" The world, and the things that are in it, will one day, like an Arab's tent, be folded away. There is nothing that endures but God!

And as He went about preaching, He taught the lesson of the Divine Sense of Humor, and He never took anything seriously except the soul. He saw the fishermen gathering in their nets but He did not take them seriously: to Him they were fishers of men. The pearl was not to be taken seriously, for thanks to the Divine Sense of Humor, the pearl was the worth of faith and grace. The quickness of the lightning flash from east to west was not just a physical phenomena to be taken seriously: to Him it was the revelation of the quickness of judgment. A wedding garment was not to be taken seriously (although June brides do take it seriously), a wedding garment was a revelation of charity. And so on all through His life every material thing He viewed as a telltale of some great eternal lesson. Every trivial incident was

69

a symbol of God's working among men. The fishes of the sea, the birds of the air that reap not nor sow, the lilies of the field arrayed in garments more glorious than Solomon, camels and eyes of needles, gardens and husbandmen, thorns and thistles, bread and serpents, sheep and goats, wheat and chaff, hen and chickens, and all other parables of His ministry—all these seemingly insignificant things of ordinary life were to Him as transparent as the very air, and each and every one of them contained within itself a marvelous and wonderful lesson about the goodness of God, but only those who had a Divine Sense of Humor could see through things as He did, and read their lesson. The serious can never speak in parables, because the parables are for only those with a sense of the invisible.

He never stood in the midst of His creation looking menially down upon the grass that is trod under the feet, as something utterly beneath and below Him. It was as if every time He looked into the heart of a rose, He felt that He was in the presence of His Invisible Father Who, though concealing His wise hand, was touching the rose with His invisible brush, and though concealing, His mind was nevertheless giving it a form and a beauty that leaves all other beauty pain.

Such is the history of the Divine Sense of Humor, and now that we know what it is, we may ask who are they who understand and comprehend it. I believe that there are two classes of people in the world who have understood the new vision of things that our Divine Lord brought to earth, namely, poets and saints.

Poets are those who have been richly endowed with a sense of the invisible, who can look out upon exactly the same phenomena that other mortals take seriously, and see in them something of the Divine. All of us look out upon the sunrise and the sunset, but it is only a poet endowed with the Divine Sense of Humor like Francis Thompson who can speak of the day as a priest and the sun as a Host, and then thrill us with the thought that each morning the priest goes to the orient tabernacle, from it he takes the host, and lifts It in benediction high over the world, and then at night sets It in the flaming monstrance of the west. The world invisible he saw; the world

71

intangible he touched; the world inapprehen-
sible he clutched; and in the world in which he
moved, one needed only to move a stone to start
a wing, and to look out upon the waters, not
of Genesreth, but Thames, to see Christ walking there in the glory of the morning sunrise.

It is only a poet like Joyce Kilmer, endowed
with a like sense of the invisible, that could see
in the branches of the trees arms outstretched
in prayer, and in all the red blood and horror
of war, a Divine Lesson. As he marched and
trod though the muddy fields, carrying a rifle
and a pack, he saw in it all, thanks to his Divine
Sense of Humor, the story of another Man and
another burden.

My shoulders ache beneath my pack
   (Lie easier, Cross, upon His back).

I march with feet that burn and smart
   (Tread, Holy Feet, upon my heart).

Men shout at me who may not speak
   (They scourged Thy back and smote Thy cheek).

I may not lift a hand to clear
My eyes of salty drops that sear.

   (Then shall my fickle soul forget
Thy Agony of Bloody Sweat?)

72

My rifle hand is stiff and numb
  (From Thy pierced palm red rivers come).

Lord, Thou didst suffer more for me
Than all the hosts of land and sea.

So let me render back again
This millionth of Thy gift. Amen.[1]

A similar vision of things has come to another man of faith, Joseph Mary Plunkett, who met his untimely brave death in Ireland not many years ago. This young Irish soul saw the same fields and rivers and roses that others see. But he also saw through them and, thanks to his Divine Sense of Humor, he could write:

I see His blood upon the rose
And in the stars, the glory of His eyes,
His body gleams amid eternal snows,
His tears fall from the skies.

I see His face in every flower,
The thunder and the singing of the birds are but His
     voice—
And carven by His power
Rocks are His written words.

And pathways by His Feet are worn,
His strong heart stirs the ever-beating sea,
His crown of thorns is twined with every thorn,
His cross is every tree.[2]

[1] Joyce Kilmer, "The Prayer of a Soldier in France."
[2] Joseph Mary Plunkett, "I See His Blood upon the Rose."

When one hears such thoughts as these, one can hardly ever think of any other name for a Christian poet except to say that he is a "marred saint."

The other class of people who have the Divine Sense of Humor are saints. I do not mean canonized saints, but rather that great army of stanch and solid Christians to whom everything and every incident speaks a story of God's love. A saint can be defined as one who has a Divine Sense of Humor, for a saint never takes this world seriously as the lasting city. To him the world is like a scaffolding up through which souls climb to the Kingdom of Heaven, and when the last soul shall have climbed up through it, then it shall be torn down and burned with a fervent fire, not because it is base, but simply because it has done its work —it has brought souls back again to God. A saint is one who looks out upon this world as a nursery to the Father's heavenly mansion and a stepping-stone to the Kingdom of Heaven. A saint is one to whom everything in the world is a sacrament. In the strict sense of the term, there are only seven sacraments, but in the broad sense of the term everything in the world is a sacrament, for everything in the world can be used as a means of special sanctification. A saint is one who never complains about the particular duty of his state in life, for he knows full well that "all the world's a stage, and all the men and women merely players." Why, then, should he who plays the part of a king glory in his tinsel crown and tin sword, and believe that he is better than some one else who plays the part of a peasant, for when the curtain goes down they are all men? So, too, why should any one, who in this world happens to enjoy either the accident of honor or wealth, believe he is better than some one else who may possess neither gold nor worldly learning? Why should he glory in his tinseled crown and tin sword, and believe that he is better than some one else who plays a less important rôle in the great drama of life? For when the curtain goes down on the last day, and we respond to the curtain call of judgment, we will not be asked what part we played, but how well we played the part that was assigned to us.

A saint, then, is one who has learned to spiritualize and sacramentalize and ennoble everything in the world, and make of it a prayer. No occupation is too base for such spiritualization, nor is any suffering too hard for such ennobling. It is only those who have not this highly developed sense that let the opportunities of daily life pass by without either making of them a prayer, or drawing from them a divine lesson. Centuries ago according to a story perhaps apocryphal, in the streets of Florence there stood a beautiful piece of Carrara marble that had been cut and hacked and ruined by some cheap artist. Other mediocre artists passed it by, and bemoaned that it should have been so ruined. One day Michelangelo passed it by, asked that it be brought to his studio. He there applied to it his chisel, his genius, and his inspiration. He drew out of it the immortal statue of David. The lesson contained herein is that there is nothing so base or low that it cannot be reconquered, that there is no duty however menial that cannot be retrieved for sanctity, and that there is nothing that is cast down that cannot be lifted up.

Down in the gutter of a city street was a drop of water, soiled, dirty, and stagnant. Way up in the heavens a gentle sunbeam saw it, leaped out its azure sky, down to the drop, kissed it, thrilled it through and through with new strange life and hope, and lifted it up higher and higher and higher, beyond the clouds, and one day let it fall as a flake of immaculate snow on a mountaintop. And so our own lives—humdrum, routine, tiresome lives of a workaday world—can be ennobled, spiritualized, and sacramentalized, provided we bring to them the inspiration of Some One who saw apostolic zeal in salt, provided we infuse their carbon blackness with the electric flame of love which will make them glow with the brilliance of a diamond, provided we bring to them the inspiration of the great Captain who carries five wounds in the forefront of battle, and thrills them with the fixed flash of the lightning made eternal as the Light.

And when we have done this, then perhaps we will understand why He who came to this earth to teach us the Divine Sense of Humor showed us everything that was lovely and beautiful in His character—except one thing. He showed us His power; He showed us His wisdom; He showed us His melting kindness; He showed us His sorrow; He showed us His tears; He showed us His forgiveness; He showed us His power over nature; He showed us His knowledge of human hearts; but there was one thing that He did not show; there was one thing He saved for those who do not take this world too seriously; there was one thing He saved for Paradise; there was one thing He saved for those who, like poets and saints, have a Divine Sense of Humor; there was one thing He saved for heaven that will make heaven heaven, and that was—His smile!

THE FREEDOM OF AUTHORITY

STEVENSON once said that not on bread alone doth man live, but principally on catchwords. High-sounding phrases often go rattling by like express-trains, carrying the burden of those who are too lazy to think for themselves. Among these phrases or catchwords there is none in the field of religion which has greater modern appeal than the one: "The modern man wants a religion of the spirit, and not a religion of authority." Years ago its popular expression was that "we must be free from the slavery of Rome." To-day it is more direct: "No Catholic can be free because he is bound down by law and authority."

There is no doubting the sincerity of those who accept such catchwords: hence there can be no doubt that they will accept a sincere explanation of the teaching of the church concerning authority, law, and freedom which for the sake of clearness may be set down in the three following propositions: first, the necessity of law and authority; secondly, obedience to highest law and authority constitutes freedom; thirdly, the obedience to the law and authority of the Church is thrilling and romantic.

First: It is false to say that we can be absolutely free from law and authority, for freedom from law and authority is an illusion. The real problem is not whether we will accept law and authority, but rather, which law and authority we will accept. Even though this is a free country, I find that if I do not obey the authority of my government, then I shall have to accept the authority of a warden; if I do not accept the authority of the pure-food commission, then I shall have to accept the authority of the undertaker; if I do not accept the authority of the traffic lights, I shall have to accept the authority of the jailer. In religious matters, if I do not accept the authority of the Church, then I must accept the authority of public opinion. Public opinion is the common stalk of thought and sentiment created by human society, and in the realm of religion outside the Church it is practically always a compromise.

Modern religion affirms just as much of spiritual and moral truth as in a given condition will keep society together—just so much and no more. It affirms not the whole law of God, but extracts from it, and only those extracts which seem to be most useful for social purposes, and of which society itself will approve. For example, at the present time it dilates on the Sermon on the Mount, but says absolutely nothing about the Last Judgment. It quotes, "Behold the lilies of the field," but never the text, "What exchange shall a man give for his soul?" Again, modern religion sternly condemns murder and punishes it by death, and all this in strict accordance with the Divine Law: but it also permits divorce and marriage after divorce, a proceeding which Our Blessed Lord, in very express terms, condemned as adulterous and wrong. In other words, modern religion has approved one aspect of the Divine Law concerning murder, and disapproved another, concerning divorce. The reason it does this is because public opinion believes murder to be destructive of society, but does not believe that divorce can be equally destructive of it in the long run. Religion thus compromises, or strikes an average between what is good and what is bad. It approves

83

Christ only inasmuch as Christ approves it. It accepts His teachings and His authority only inasmuch as its maxims and its opinions approve those teachings.

Hence, the problem confronting the religious man of to-day is not whether he will obey or disobey law and authority; but, which of the two he will obey, namely, the authority of public opinion, or the authority of Christ and tradition. And all thinking men, as a celebrated English essayist has put it, want a religion to-day which is right, not when the world is right, but is right when the world is wrong, and by this he meant the authority of the Church which holds to the teachings of Christ, even though public opinion should cry out for the liberation of Barabbas, for the Church is built solidly upon the conviction that right is right if nobody's right, and wrong is wrong if everybody's wrong.

Furthermore, and here we pass on to the second point, only by obedience to the highest law and authority does a man become free. Let me give a few examples to prove this point. A dictionary represents a standard in the use of words. It is a court of appeal, or an authority concerning their meaning. Now it is only by submitting to authority that I ever become free to use words. I may use the word "moon" and by it mean "cabbage"; I may use the word "cow," and by it mean "cowslip." I soon find, however, that I am no longer free to tell my fellow-man the story that the cow jumped over the moon. It is only by submission to law and authority that we ever become free.

Or, to take an example from the realm of arts. If an artist, in a fever of broadmindedness and a desire to be free, chooses to paint a giraffe with a short neck, he will soon discover that he will not be free to paint a giraffe at all. If in a feverish love for the new art of self-expression which obeys no law, he decides to paint a zebra without stripes, and a leopard without spots, and a triangle with four sides, he will soon discover that he is not free at all to paint even zebras, leopards, or triangles. It is only by obedience to law and authority and the inherent nature of things that we ever become free. Now man has a rational nature which means that the law of his being is practical reason or conscience. Only inasmuch as man obeys the dictates of his conscience is he free to be a man. He may choose to disobey his conscience, and he is free to become an animal, but he is not free to be a man.

A final example in the field of science: imagine a railroad locomotive, endowed with consciousness, so that it is able to read, to think, to speak. And supposing that one day it picked up with its cow-catcher one of the modern books on the morality of self-expression, such as one of Mr. Bertrand Russell's, in which he rebels against obedience to traditional moral laws, and the authority of Christian teaching. And suppose, with its great single cyclops eye, it reads the pages of this liberal thinker, and becomes so impressed with its fine sophistic idioms that it whistles to itself, "Mr. Russell is right. What do the engineers who designed me and imposed their laws upon me know about my inner impulses? Why should I even obey the authority of an engineer who is constantly limiting my steam pressure to one hundred pounds a square inch, when I have the vital Freudian urge to make it one hundred and fifty pounds? And, furthermore, why should I submit myself to the authority of railroad officials who, fifty years ago, laid the tracks upon which

I should run? Why should I take this curve, that straightaway, this bridge, simply because they decided over two score years ago that I should? Why should I not be permitted to choose my own directions, and to make my own tracks? From now on, I am going to be free. From now on I am going to be self-expressive!"

Suppose the locomotive did become so self-expressive. In refusing to obey the laws concerning steam pressure, it would discover it was no longer free to be a locomotive, because in asserting its pressure beyond the normal, it would burst its entrails; secondly, by refusing to keep on the track it would no longer be free to run. And if the locomotive did jump the track, and burst its boilers, it would not hurt the engineer who designed the track; it would hurt only itself. And so, too, if a man disobeys God's laws, and dashes his head against them, as against an eternal rock, the rock does not suffer—it is only the head of the man that suffers.

Finally, it is only by obedience to the laws of Christ and His Church that we ever become free. And obedience to this authority is positively thrilling, for all orthodoxy is romantic.

If there is any vision or mental picture to be had at all of the condition of the world a few centuries ago and now, it might be the vision of a great rocky island in the very center of a stormy and raging sea. Previous to the break-up of Christian unity three centuries ago, this island may be represented as surrounded by a great stone wall against which the waves spent their fury, but never broke it down. Inside the wall were thousands and thousands of the children of God playing games, singing songs, and enjoying life, to the utter oblivion of the great devouring sea outside. With the dawning of the day of False Freedom, there came to the island a group of men who argued with the children in some such language as this: "Why have you permitted the Church of Rome to surround you with all her laws and dogmas? Can you not see that she has encompassed you, and has not permitted you to think for yourself or to be free and captains of your own fate? Tear down the walls! Break down the barriers! Throw off the obstacles and learn to be free!" And the children tore down the walls. One day I went back and I saw all the children huddled together in the center of the island, afraid to move, afraid to play, afraid to dance, afraid of falling into the sea.

We who, by the Grace of God, have been blessed with the protection of the Church's law and authority, can never quite understand why any one can ever think that obedience to that law and authority is enslaving. On the contrary, it is positively romantic. The laws and doctrines of the Church are not dams which stop up the river of Thought; they are levees which prevent that river from overflowing the country-side. They are not wrenches thrown into the machinery of life, but oils which make it run more smoothly. It is easy to fall into the excesses of the modern world, just as it is easy to fall off a log. It is easy to float down stream with the popular fancies—even dead bodies can float down stream. But it is exhilarating to fight against the current.

It is easy to be an atheist, and to say the world does not require a God, just as it is easy to be a pantheist, and say that the world is God; but it is thrilling to walk between those two abysses and hold that God is in the world, but not of it—and such is the Incarnation. It would be easy to fall into the extreme of the Stoics,

89

and say that pain is the law of life, or to fall into the equally stupid extreme of saying pleasure is the law of life, but it is romantic to escape the pitfalls and hold that pain is the prelude to life—and such is the lesson of Easter.

It would be easy to say with Gandhi that life should be a fast, just as it would be easy to say with the pagan that it should be a feast; but it is thrilling to avoid both extremes, and hold that the fast should precede the feast. Every heresy in the history of the Church has been either a truth exaggerated to an excess, or diminished to a defect. Calvinism, for example, had a very good first principle, which is a sound Catholic principle, namely, the absolute Sovereignty of God; but Calvin carried it so far as to rule out human merit. Bolshevism, too, is grounded on a very sound Catholic principle, which is the Brotherhood of Man, but it has exaggerated it so far as to leave no room for the Sovereignty of God. And so it is easy to fall into any of these extremes, and to lose one's intellectual balance. The thrill is in keeping it.

In other words, the Church is not so much to be compared with the Niagara Falls, as it is to be compared with a great and tremendous Rock weighing ten thousand tons, which is poised on another rock by the delicate balance of no more than six inches of a base. Niagara is a falls, simply because it cannot help falling; it is the easiest thing to do; it is simply letting things go. But that great Rock, which is pitched on a base no bigger than one's hand, has a thousand angles at which it will fall, but there is only one on which it will stand, and it is that which makes falling a far more serious thing than the falling and churning of all of Niagara's waters. And so with the Church. All through her history she has been like that great Rock, poised on the very brink of an abyss, and it is that which has made her romantic; for danger is the root and foundation of all romance in drama.

Why do children like to play robber, walk picket fences, tramp into thick woods, play along banks of deep rivers, throw stones at vicious dogs, listen to blood-curdling ghost stories, walk on roofs? Is it not because each and every child has deep-rooted in his heart as the foundation for his manhood, and as the very condition for his enjoying life, the love of danger and the thrill of being near it, and yet never falling completely into it? Why do children, when they grow up into man's estate, love to play games of chance, hunt wild beasts, explore the icy extremities of the earth, fly over trackless seas, speed at the rate of four miles a minute over land, and five miles a minute in the air; if it is not because they, too, love the thrill that comes with danger, and love still more the glorious escape from that to which they had so often exposed themselves? And what is true of children and true of men, is true of the Church. It is extremely thrilling to belong to the Church. It is exhilarating to be orthodox. It is romantic to be poised on the Rock of Peter that could fall into a thousand pitfalls, and yet never falls.

Every person has an instinctive desire to witness a storm at sea, providing he could be sure of reaching port. We who ride in Peter's bark witness such a storm, and know we will reach port. For twenty centuries the bark of Peter has been riding, riding the seas, and for twenty centuries we who have been on board know the romance of the seas and its dangers, but also the romance of a port. Sometimes that bark has come within a hair's breadth of dashing against the rocks, of saying that Christ was man and not God, and then again it has suddenly had to swerve to avoid crashing into the opposite rock and saying that Christ is God but not man. At other moments in her voyage, Peter's bark has come within a razor's edge of being stranded on the sands of humanism and saying that man does everything, and God does nothing. And then, by an equally dexterous move, she saves herself from the sand-bars of declaring with the oriental mystics that God does everything and man does nothing. It would have been extremely easy for Peter and his successors to have sunk their ship in the depths of determinism, just as it would have been very easy for the ship to have capsized in the shallow waters of sentimentalism in the twentieth century. But it is wonderfully thrilling to have avoided both. It would have been very easy for the bark of Peter to have been lost in the fogs of Modernism, just as it would have been easy for it to have lost its course in the mists of Fundamentalism. But to have avoided both of these snares, not by mere chance, but by intellectual direction, is thrill-

ing. If one small blunder, concerning the doctrine of original sin, were made in her twenty
centuries of charting the course of men to God,
huge blunders would have been made in human happiness. A mistranslation of a single
word one thousand years ago, might have
smashed all the statues of Europe. A false
move in the Council of the Vatican might have
impoverished reason. By one single slip, the
Church might have stopped all the dances,
withered all the Christmas trees, and broken
all the Easter eggs.

But the Church has avoided all these pitfalls
and all these errors, and as the bark of Peter,
with sails flying high, cuts the waters of the
sea, she looks before and aft. Behind her she
can see the shriveled hulks of a thousand her-
esies and mental fashions that were suited to
their times and died because that is all they
were suited for—their times. Before her she can
see the shipwrecked rafts of Masterless men
looking for the Master Peter who is not for one
time but all time. And now its future will be
just as thrilling as the past. Always in danger,
always escaping it; always threatened, always
conquering; always enjoying the romance of

avoiding extremes, the bark is destined to go on through all the storms and tempests of the world, until one day it checks pace at the hid battlements of eternity, and there as the children disembark from the ship of Peter, they will understand why it avoided the snares and pitfalls—because as Peter stood at the helm of his bark, there rested on his hands the invisible, eternal hands of Christ, whom the winds and seas obey; Christ, who steers the sun and moon and stars in their courses.

MOTHER AND BABE

CHRISTMAS is the season in which eyes and hearts are drawn in memory and in love to a Babe who was born in a cave under the floor of the world, the Babe whose birth shook the world to its very foundations. It is the hour of the stupendous mystery of Omnipotence wrapped in swaddling bands and laid in a manger. Divinity is always where the world least expects to find it. No one in the world ever would have thought that He who threw the fiery ball of the sun into the heavens, would one day be warmed by the breath of oxen. No one in the world would ever have suspected that hands which could tumble planets and worlds into space, would one day be smaller than the huge heads of the cattle. No one in the world would ever have thought that He who could make for Himself a canopy of stars, would one day be covered by the roof of a stable. And yet such are the ways of God. In order to confound the power of the world He comes in the weakness of a child, and in order to set at naught its pride, He makes His bed in straw. He made the world as His Home, and then on the first Christmas Day He decided to come into it, but the world received Him not, and thus the story of Christmas is the story of a God who was homeless at Home.

But while we pay this primary act of adoration to the God who brought heaven to earth, there is danger that some of us may forget just how the Child came into the world: in fact, certain modern forms of Christianity speak of the Babe but never a word about the Mother of the Babe. The Babe of Bethlehem did not fall from the heavens into a bed of straw, but came into this world through the great portals of the flesh. Sons are inseparable from mothers, and mothers inseparable from sons. Just as you cannot go to a statue of a mother holding a babe, and cut away the mother, leaving the babe suspended in mid-air, neither can you cleave away the Mother from the Babe of Bethlehem. He was not suspended mid-air in history, but like all other babes, came into the world by and through His mother. While we adore the Child, should we not then venerate His

Mother, and while we kneel to Jesus, should we not at least clasp the hand of Mary for giving us such a Saviour? There is a grave danger that, lest in celebrating a Christmas without the Mother, we may soon reach a point where we will celebrate Christmas without the Babe, and these days are upon us now. And what an absurdity that would be; for, just as there can never be a Christmas without a Christ, so there can never be a Christ without a Mary.

Pull aside the curtain of the past, and under the light of Revelation discover the rôle and interpret the part that Mary plays in the great Drama of Redemption!

Almighty God never launches a great work without exceeding preparation. The two greatest works of God are the Creation of the first man, Adam, and the Incarnation of the Son of God, the new Adam, Jesus Christ. But neither of these was accomplished without characteristic Divine preparation.

God did not make the masterpiece of creation, which was man, on the very first day, but deferred it until He had labored for six days in ornamenting the universe. From no material thing, but only by the fiat of His Will, Omnip-

101

otence moved and said to Nothingness, "Be"; and lo and behold spheres fell into their orbits passing one another in beautiful harmony without ever a hitch or a halt. Then came the living things: the herbs bearing fruit as unconscious tribute to their Maker; the trees, with their leafy arms outstretched all day in prayer; and the flowers opening the chalice of their perfumes to their Creator. With the labor that was never exhausting, God then made the sensitive creatures to roam about, either in the watery palaces of the depths, or on wings, to fly through trackless space, or else as unwinged to roam the fields in search of their repast and natural happiness. But all of this beauty, which has inspired the song of poets and the tracings of artists, was not in the Divine Mind sufficiently beautiful for the creature whom God would make the lord and master of the universe. He would do one thing more: He would set apart as a choice garden, a small portion of His creation, beautify it with four rivers flowing through lands rich with gold onyx, permit to roam in it the beasts of the field as domestics of that garden, in order to make it a paradise of the most intense happiness and pleasure pos-

sible to earth. When finally that Eden was made
beautiful, as only God knows how to make
things beautiful, He launched further the masterpiece of His creation, which was the first
man, and in that paradise of pleasure was celebrated the first nuptials of humanity—the union of flesh and flesh of the first man and
woman, Adam and Eve.

Now if God so prepared for His first great
work which was man, by making the Paradise
of Creation, it was even more fitting that before
sending His Son to redeem the world, He
should prepare for Him a Paradise of the Incarnation. And for four thousand years He prepared it by symbols and then prophecies. In
the language of types He prepared human
minds for some understanding of what this
new Paradise would be. The burning bush of
Moses inundated with the glory of God, and
conserving in the midst of its flame the fresh-
ness of its verdure and the perfume of its flowers, was a symbol of a new Paradise conserving in the honor of its maternity the very
perfume of virginity. The rod of Aaron flourish-
ing in the solitude of the temple while isolated
from the world by silence and retreat, was a

symbol of that Paradise which, in a place of retirement and isolation from the world, would engender the very flower of the human race. The Ark of alliance, where the tables of the law were conserved, was a symbol of the new Paradise in which the Law in the Person of Christ would take up His very residence.

God prepared for that Paradise, not only by symbols, but also by prophecies. Even in that dread day when an angel with a flaming sword was stationed in the first garden in creation, a prophecy was made that the serpent would not eventually conquer, but that a woman would crush its head. Later on Isaias and Jeremias hailed that holy Paradise as one which would encircle a man.

But prophets and symbols were a too distant preparation. God would labor still more on His Paradise. He would make a Paradise not overrun with weeds and thistles, but blooming with every flower of virtue; a Paradise at the portals of which sin had never knocked, nor against the gates of which infidelity would never dare to storm; a Paradise from which would flow not four rivers through lands rich with gold and onyx, but four oceans of grace to the four corners of the world; a Paradise destined to bring forth the Tree of Life, and therefore, full of life and grace itself; a Paradise in which was to be tabernacled Purity itself, and therefore one immaculately pure; a Paradise so beautiful and sublime that the Heavenly Father would not have to blush in sending His Son into it. That Paradise of the Incarnation to be gardenered by the Adam new, that flesh-girt Paradise in which there were to be celebrated the nuptials, not of man and woman, but of humanity and divinity, is Our Own Beloved Mary, Mother of Our Lord and Saviour, Jesus Christ.

And thus, as we gather about the crib of Bethlehem, we somehow feel that we are in the presence of a new Paradise of Beauty and Love and Innocence, and the name of that Paradise is Mary. God labored for six days and produced Eden for the first Adam; now He labored anew, and produced the new Eden, Mary, for the new Adam, Christ. And if we could have been there in that stable on that first Christmas night, we might have seen that Paradise of the Incarnation, but we should not be able to recollect whether her face was beautiful or not, nor should we be able to recall any of her features, for what would have impressed us, and made us forget all else, would have been the lovely sinless soul that shone through her eyes like two celestial suns, that spoke in her mouth which only breathed in prayer, the soul that was heard in her voice, which was like the hushed song of the angels. If we could have stood before that Paradise we would have less peered at it, as into it, for what would have impressed us would not have been any external quality, though such would have been ravishing, but rather the qualities of her soul—her simplicity, innocence, humility, and above all, her purity. So completely would all these qualities have possessed our soul, like so much divine music, that our first thought would have been, "Oh! So beautiful," and our second thought would have been, "Oh! What hateful creatures we are."

Tell me why should not that Paradise of the Incarnation be spotless and pure? Why should she not be immaculate and stainless? Just suppose that you could have preëxisted your own mother, in much the same way that an artist preëxists his painting. Furthermore, suppose

that you had an infinite power to make your
mother anything that you pleased, just as a
great artist like Raphael has the power of real-
izing his artistic ideals. Suppose you had this
double power, what kind of mother would you
have made for yourself? Would you have made
her of such a type that would make you blush
because of her unwomanly and unmotherlike
actions? Would you have in any way stained
and soiled her with the selfishness that would
make her unattractive not only to you, but to
your fellow-man? Would you have made her
exteriorly and interiorly of such a character as
to make you ashamed of her, or would you have
made her, so far as human beauty goes, the
most beautiful woman in the world; and so far
as beauty of soul goes, one who would radiate
every virtue, every manner of kindness and
charity and loveliness; one who by the purity
of her life and her mind and her heart would be
an inspiration not only to you, but even to your
fellow-men, so that all would look up to her as
the very incarnation of what is best in motherhood? Now, if you who are an imperfect being
and who have not the most delicate conception
of all that is fine in life, would have wished for

the loveliest of mothers, do you think that our Blessed Lord, who not only preëxisted His own mother, but who had an infinite power to make her just what He chose, would, in virtue of all of the infinite delicacy of His spirit make her any less pure and loving and beautiful than you would have made your own mother? If you who hate selfishness, would have made her selfless, and you who hate ugliness, would have made her beautiful, do you not think that the Son of God who hates sin would have made His own mother sinless, and He who hates moral ugliness, would have made her immaculately beautiful?

I plead, therefore, for a Christmas in which the Babe is not an Orphan, but a Child of Mary; I plead for a religion which breathes respect for Motherhood, and vibrates with a love for that Mother, above all mothers, who brought Our Saviour into the world. If there is any man or woman looking for a test as to what constitutes the divine religion on this earth, let him apply the same test he would to the judgment of a man. If you ever want to know the real qualities of a man, judge him not by his attitude to the world of commerce, his out-

108

look on business, his kindness and his genteel manners, but judge him rather by his attitude to his own mother. If you want to know the quality of a religion, judge it exactly the same way, that is, not by the way it seeks to please men, but rather by the attitude that it bears to the Mother of Our Blessed Lord. If you find a religion which never speaks of that Woman who gave us our Redeemer; a religion which in its liturgy and its devotions, is silent about that most beautiful of women; and in its history has even broken her images and statues, then there certainly must be something wanting to the truth of that religion, and let me add, even to its humanity.

Our Blessed Lord could hardly be expected to look with favor on those who forgot His Mother, who nourished Him as a Babe, carried Him into Egypt, caressed Him as a Child, and stood at the bedside of the Cross when, with almost His last breath, He tenderly called her "Mother." Really one of the great inconsistencies of the modern world is its sentimental and almost commercial attachment to "Mother's Day," and its complete forgetfulness of the Mother of mothers, the Mother of Our

109

Lord, and the Mother of men, without whom all motherhood lacks a Christian ideal. I can understand why a man should love his mother, but I cannot understand why a man who calls himself a Christian and a follower of Christ should not have a very deep and intense love for His own Mother. I repeat, therefore, that a quick test for the divinity of any religion is its outlook on the motherhood of Christ. And if you want to know just how intense and deep and loyal our love is to that sweet Mother, then place your hands over our heart.

Christmas takes on a new meaning when the Mother is seen with the Babe. In fact, the heavens and the earth seem almost to exchange places. Years and years ago, aye! centuries ago, we used to think of heaven as "way up there." Then one day, the God of heavens came to this earth, and at that hour when Mary held the Babe in her arms, it became true to say that with her we now "look down" to Heaven.

In these days when Mother is separated from her Child, which is Birth Control, and a husband is separated from his wife, which is Divorce, we plead for the return of the Ideal Mother and we address her:

With our forlorn and cheerless condition, Sweet Queen, we pray thee, give us patience and endurance. When our spirit is exalted or depressed, when it loses its balance, when it is restless or wayward, when it is sick of what it has and hankers after what it has not, when our mortal frame trembles under the shadow of the tempter, we shall call on Thee, and ask Thee to bring us back to ourselves, for Thou art the cool breath of the immaculate, the fragrance of the rose of Sharon—Thou art the Paradise of the Incarnation—Thou art Our Queen—Our Mother—Our Immaculate Mother, and we love Thee!

THE ONLY THING THAT MATTERS

THE ONLY THING THAT MATTERS

THE utterly disillusioned man, uprooted from the past and disinherited by tradition, is wandering about the modern Babylon, and like a man who knows not where he is going, pictures to himself a thousand destinations. Like a drowning man who has lost his hold on final truths, he clutches first at this philosophy and that theory, only to discover them to be as helpless as straw. He seeks refuge in a humanistic outlook, and takes pride in the progress of civilization, and yet down in his heart knows that he is confusing comfort with civilization, and change with progress. His moral nature he knows to be crude and nothing more than a mass of likes and dislikes, and a jumble of prejudices and prepossessions. Possessed of no other standards than comfort and seemliness, and though boastful of modern education, he will secretly avow that never before were there so many scholars and so little scholarship, so many wise men and so little wisdom.

The World War, which every man feels he is still fighting, has left not only chaos, but also the uncertainty of minds confronted by chaos. The ephemeral theorists are in the saddle; the wisdom of the centuries is crying alone in the wilderness; and the Church is ignored, for, "can anything of good come from Nazareth?" A pessimistic despair, a melancholic sex-madness has made of the modern man a victim of the need to believe. He may go on trying fool theories, and he probably will, until he returns to the father's house which his forefathers left in the sixteenth century. It will be only there that he will find rest, for what the modern man needs is an infusion of new blood. He needs a cross-fertilization with eternity, and to help him discover himself, we have set down the Catholic philosophy of life in which are indicated the stepping-stones to those great peaks. The steps are three-fold: first, silence; secondly, reflection; and thirdly, primacy of the spiritual.

Silence: One of the really great needs of our own day is silence. Modern life seems to thrive on a fondness for noise, and by noise I mean not only the staccato barbarism of jazz, or the

116

bleating and moaning of saxophone orchestras, but also, and principally, the excessive desire for that which distracts—love of amusements, constant goings and comings, excitements and thrills, and movement for the mere sake of movement. What is the reason of this fondness for noise? It is not due to any inherent love of that which is loud, for people generally prefer that which is soft and refined. Rather the reason is to be found in the great desire on the part of human beings to do the impossible, namely—to escape from themselves. They do not like to be with themselves because they are not pleased with themselves; they do not like to be alone with their conscience, because their conscience reproves and carries on an unbearable repartee. They do not like to be quiet, because the footsteps of the Hound of Heaven which can be heard in silence, cannot be heard in the din of excitement; they do not like to be silent, because God's voice is like a whisper and it cannot be heard in the tumult of the city streets. These are some of the reasons why the modern world loves noise, and they are all resolvable to this: noise drowns God's voice and stupefies conscience. Dull, indeed, are these

117

distractions, but like the clay used by savages to dull the pain of hunger, they stifle in the soul the hunger for the presence of God. The result is that very few people ever know themselves. In fact, they know every one else better than they know themselves. That is why so few ever see their own faults.

> The world is too much with us late and soon;
> Getting and spending we lay waste our powers;
> Little we use in nature that is ours;
> We have given our souls away—a sordid boon.
>
> See all the sights from pole to pole,
> And glance and nod and bustle by;
> And never once possess our soul,
> Before we die.[1]

In order to remedy this condition, what is needed is less amusing and more musing; a silence; a going apart into the desert of our souls to rest a while; a solitariness from men, and an aloneness with God; a quiet which permits the soul to be sensitive to the whispers of God; a requiem or a rest from modern maxims and the excuses of new philosophies and the excitements which appeal to the body and disturb

[1] William Wordsworth, "The World Is Too Much with Us."

the soul; a privacy inspired by the example of
Him who needed least of all mankind a preparation of silence for a life of activity, and yet
had the greatest of them all; a tranquillity inspired by Him who in the midst of a busy life
spent whole nights on mountaintops in prayer.

Silence is the condition of entering into oneself, which is another way of saying, of finding
God. Within our own time two great men of
activity, Charles de Foucault and Ernest
Pschiari, the grandson of Renan, soldiers of
France, men of dissipation, both were brought
to the very threshold of sanctity by the silence
of the Eastern skies, where stars seem so close
that one could almost reach up and pluck them
out of the heavens. Foucault died as a priest,
perhaps massacred for his faith by the Moham-
medans, and Pschiari was killed during the
World War; and yet both came to Christ
through the repose and quiet forced upon them
by their life in the French Legion. We cannot
travel to the quiet of the Oriental skies, but we
need not; for silence is not dependent upon a
place, but upon a state of mind; it is not based
on where we are, but what we are thinking
about. It is being alone as far as the world is

concerned, even though one is in the very midst of it—an activity by which every faculty of the heart and mind and soul is bent inward, awaiting the voice of God.

Reflection: Silence constitutes the environment of the second effect of entering into ourselves, namely, reflection. In moments of silence, men begin to seek God. The self-conscious spirit emerges from the flux of life and in contemplation and reflection finds itself dissatisfied with what it has, and hankers after what it has not. The soul begins to part company with animal desires, and begins at least a blundering search for the hiding place of that haunting presence which seems to speak to him from every burning bush. The embryonic instinct for heaven now cries out for its object, and as the vague sense of unexplained powers conditions it, reflection begins, and reflection means asking oneself the question, "Why am I here?" and finding the answer in the words of the penny catechism, "To know, love and serve God, in this world, and be happy with Him forever in the next."

Suppose I stopped a clerk, a banker, a merchant, a messenger-boy, on the way to work to-morrow morning, and suppose I put to them the question, "Whither are you going?" They would answer, "To my labor." "But, why do you labor?" "I labor to earn a reward." "But suppose I told you that a very wealthy man had died and left an immense fortune to all who labor; would you be interested in knowing the conditions upon which that fortune might be yours?"

There is not one who would refuse. And yet, Almighty God has Himself promised a heavenly reward to all men who labor. Why are they not interested in learning something of its conditions? Why are they not concerned in discovering the ways and means to its possession? If we are concerned with an earthly reward, why should we not be concerned with a heavenly reward? If we are concerned with a temporal livelihood, why should we not be concerned with an Eternal Life? What, after all, is the use of amassing wealth, if God is going to require our soul? Our shrouds will have no pockets. Was not this the point in the parable of the man who filled his barns? He added store to store, building to building, and in our own language, dollar to dollar, and then said to his

121

soul, "Soul, thou hast much goods laid up for many years. Take thy rest: eat, drink, make good cheer." But God said to him, "Thou fool! This night do they require thy soul of thee, and whose shall those things be which thou hast provided?" "So is he that layeth up treasure for himself and is not rich towards God." Reflection on such a parable convinces the soul that the great idea, after all, is not the question which is so often asked by the modern world on the occasion of a death, "What did he leave behind?" but rather, "What did he take with him?" for it is only good works that follow.

The answer to the question of destiny is: that I have been made to know, love, and serve God for all eternity. Just as there are heavenly bodies which can complete their orbits only after the lapse of ages, and which then reappear with unfailing precision at the point from which they started, as if to present themselves once more to Him who sent them on their way, so, too, each soul that is sent into this world from that great white throne of God, to run its course over a brief span of years in this cosmos of ours, is destined to reappear once again before Him who sent it on its way, freighted with

122

virtues and loaded with the precious cargo of merits, to receive the crown He made for it on the day of its birth.

What is my destiny? If the experience of my daily life cries out for something beyond this world, and if there is nothing of this world that I can take with me, then my destiny must be in some way to return again to God through Christ. Then there comes over the soul that which may be called the fear of the best, that which makes us at times even want to flee the very love of God. We are afraid that if we have God we "must have naught else beside." There is the dull suspicion that Christ means sacrifice and giving up things. Then there begins the struggle of whether we shall follow our lower impulses or the higher; an angel seems to have us by the hand, and a devil by our heart. The moment on which eternity depends has come, and there probably goes on in our conquering soul some such thoughts as these:

Oh, tempt me not! I love too well this snare
    Of silken cords.
Nay, Love, the flesh is fair;
    So tempt me not! This earth affords
        Too much delight;

123

Withdraw Thee from my sight,
Lest my weak soul break free
And throw me back on Thee!

Thy face is all too marred. Nay, Love, not I—
I did not that! Doubtless Thou hadst to die;
    Others did faint for Thee; but I faint not.
    Only a little while hath sorrow got
The better of me now; for Thou art grieved,
    Thinking I need Thee. Oh, Christ, lest I fall
    Weeping between Thy Feet, and give Thee all;
Oh, Christ, lest love condemn me unreprieved
Into Thy bondage, be it not believed
    That Thou hast need of *me*!
    Dost Thou not know
    I never turned aside to mock Thy Woe?
I had respect to Thy great love for men:
Why wilt Thou, then,
    Question of each new lust—
    "Are these not ashes, and is this not dust?"

Ah, Love, Thou hast not eyes
    To see how sweet it is!
Each for himself be wise:
    Mock not my bliss!

Ere Thou cam'st troubling, was I not content?
    Because I pity Thee, and would be glad
    To go mine own way, and not leave Thee sad,
Is all my comfort spent?

Go Thine own ways, nor dream Thou needest me!
Yet, if, again, Thou on the bitter Tree

Wert hanging now, with none to succour Thee
   Or run to quench Thy sudden cry of thirst,
     Would not I be the first?—
Ah, Love, the prize!—
To lift one cloud of suffering from Thine Eyes!

   Oh, Christ, let be!
Stretch not Thine ever-pleading Hands thus wide,
Nor with imperious gesture touch Thy Side!
Past is Thy Calvary. By the Life that died,
    Oh, tempt not me!
Nay, if Thou weepest, then must I weep too,
Sweet Tempter, Christ! Yet what can *I* undo,
    I, the undone, the undone,
     To comfort Thee, God's Son?
Oh, draw me near, and, for some lowest use,
    That I may be
    Lost and undone in Thee,
Me from mine own self loose! [2]

Primacy of the Spiritual: After silence and the reflection that God is the end of all and the only peace and rest for souls, there comes the sudden and certain recognition of the primacy of the spiritual, which is the essence of the true Christian life. The primacy of the spiritual means that there is nothing in the world that really matters except the salvation of our soul, and that in its salvation the spiritual must

[2] Lawrence Housman, "Sweet Tempter Christ."

reign over the temporal, the soul over the body, grace over nature, and God over the world. Religion means this or it means nothing. This was the great emphasis of Our Lord Himself, and it therefore cannot be any less the emphasis of anything Christian. Had we been on the mountainside of Capharnaum some twenty centuries ago, mingled with the shepherd and fisherman audience of Galilee; had we felt the upland breath of that autumn evening on whose wings the great Teacher's accents rose and died away; had we marked the Eyes of Jesus, invited by the note of a bird's whirling overhead, or caught by the beauty of a distant lily floating in the Lake of Galilee, or as He pointed to the pastures brilliant with gold amaryllis, and heard the praise of the flowers that toil not; had we seen Him point to the green grass which carpets the mountainside, and heard Him draw from all the other beauties of nature lessons that Heaven tells, we should have learned that the very stars above our heads were less mysterious than the creatures below, and we should have been ashamed of our want of trust and providence in Him who made us.

One great and tremendous thought would disengage itself from His sermon on that occasion, namely, the supremacy of the world of the spirit: "Lay not up to yourselves treasures on earth: where the rust, and moth consume, and where thieves break through and steal; but lay up to yourselves treasures in heaven where neither the rust nor moth doth consume, and where thieves do not break through, nor steal. For where thy treasure is there is thy heart also. . . . You cannot serve God and Mammon. Therefore, I say to you, be not solicitous for your life, what you shall eat, nor for your body, what you shall put on. Is not the life more than the meat, and the body more than the raiment? Behold the birds of the air, for they neither sow, nor do they reap, nor gather into barns: and your Heavenly Father feedeth them. Are not you of much more value than they? And which of you, by taking thought, can add to his stature one cubit? And for raiment why are you solicitous? Consider the lilies of the field, how they grow: they labor not, neither do they spin. But I say to you, that not even Solomon in all his glory was arrayed as one of these. And if the grass of the field which is today, and tomorrow is cast into the oven, God doth so clothe: how much more you, Oh, ye of little faith? Be not solicitous, therefore, saying: 'What shall we eat: or what shall we drink, or wherewith shall we be clothed?' For after all these things do the heathens seek. For your Father knoweth that you have need of all these things. Seek ye therefore first the Kingdom of God, and His justice, and all these things shall be added unto you." .

This is an invitation to be heedless even about what we eat and drink, for in importance they are without value in relation to a soul. Such is the climax of the soul's progress to God; silence, reflection, and the primacy of the spiritual. Now cast your eye about the world, and where do you find an emphasis on the primacy of the spiritual except in the Church?

The Church is the only institution in the world to-day which is emphasizing the spiritual above all things else. That is why she scandalizes the world. That is why the pagans hate her. And despite the hate she reasserts that nothing matters in life but the salvation of a soul. That is why she builds her schools in order that children may never grow up without hearing the name of God, and in hearing, bow their knees to their Lord and Saviour. That is why she has marriage laws and insists that the faith of the Catholic party and the children born of the marriage be safeguarded; that is why she holds that if a state would command a violation of the law of God, the individual must die rather than disobey his Creator.

Consonant with this ideal, the Church holds that a tiny child who knows the existence of God and believes in the Trinity, knows far more, and is better entitled to a University degree, than professors scattered throughout the length and breadth of this land who do not know that beyond time is the Timeless, and beyond space is the Spaceless, the Infinite Lord and Master of the Universe.

The Church believes, furthermore, that a holy hour spent before the Blessed Sacrament does more good for the well-being of the world than whole days spent in talking about Progress to the utter forgetfulness of the fact that the only true Progress consists in the diminution of the traces of original sin; she believes that a penitent returning to God is of far more consequence than the return of Alsace-

129

Lorraine to France; that an increase of sancti-
fying grace in a soul is of far more value than
the increase of international credit; that a
group of cloistered nuns in prayer are more effective in preserving world peace than a group
of world politicians discussing peace to the forgetfulness of the Prince of Peace; that all the
beauties of nature do not compare in the small-
est degree with the beauty of a soul in the state
of grace; that the profoundest of scientific dis-
coveries is as naught compared with the superior intellectual intuitions of a child at its first
Communion; that the soul of a Bowery derelict
is more precious in the sight of God than the
success of any world policy; that it really does
not matter very much whether children ever
confuse Aristides with Aristotle, but it does
matter if they confuse Buddha with Christ;
that the fact that millions listen to a preacher
over the radio is of no importance whatever,
compared with a visit of a single soul to hear
the sweet whisperings of Jesus from the tabernacle; that poverty is not the greatest curse;
that physical infirmity is not the greatest ill;
that the loss of a member of a family is not so
serious as the loss of faith; that all the king-

130

doms of earth are as the least grain in the balance compared to a kingdom of a human heart in which Mary is Queen and Christ is King.

Is this excessive? Is this a loss of a sense of proportion? Is this foolishness? If it is, it is the foolishness of Our Lord: "For what shall it profit a man, if he gain the whole world, and suffer the loss of his soul?"

Every devotion to a heavenly ideal must seem foolish to a world the ideals of which are of the earth earthly. To some minds it must have seemed foolish for Our Lord on the Mount of Temptation to have repulsed Satan, when Satan, in a wild orgy of triumphant pride, revealed in all their fugitive splendor the great procession of the kingdoms of earth, and promised them to the Lord if only falling down He would adore him.

The foolishness of the Divine Founder has been the foolishness of the Divine Church. She, too, is set high on the mountaintop of the world. To that mountain, as to the Mount of Temptation, the specter of False Progress, New Freedom and Worldly Success come to her, and in vision reminds her of all the churches which would join her communion, all

131

the individuals which would join her ranks, and of all the opposition, and persecution of the world that would cease if only falling down she would adore worldly success, be a little less interested in the spiritual education of the young, a little less emphatic about the sanctity of marriage, and a little less concerned with the salvation of souls.

With the quickness of a lightning flash the Church, conscious of fellowship with her Divine Master, echoes back the words of her Master, the charter cry of spiritual freedom: "Seek ye first the kingdom of God, and His Justice."

And as the specter of Error and Worldly Success makes its way down the mountaintop, it finds at its base all the little kingdoms of passing theories and ephemeral faiths prostrate in sickening adoration before it, and in contrast to the great kingdom set high upon the mountain, the Specter of Worldly Success, like the specter of Satan, begins to realize and understand that the greatness of the world never tempts the Great—but only the small!

RELIGION WITHOUT DOGMAS

RELIGION WITHOUT DOGMAS

WHEN the hooting of owls is mistaken for the speech of philosophers, an attack on dogma is hailed as nothing short of profound and progressive wisdom. There has developed in recent years a new kind of automatic writing which afflicts principally those who write on the subject of religion. Just as soon as they take a pen in hand, they automatically write: "Religion must be free from dogmas which have fettered and hampered thinking for centuries. Religious experience, individual needs, mystic imagination—all of these must take the place of outworn creeds and dogmas. The Catholic Church, in developing dogmas and piling belief on belief, has made itself too complex, and has departed from the beautiful simplicity of the Sermon on the Mount. Our Blessed Lord," it is further argued, "never intended that there should be any iron-clad dogmas, nor that His religion should become overgrown with them."

135

The only way to determine whether Our Blessed Lord intended that His religion should have dogmas, or that it should be a matter of vague religious experience, is to go back to His very life, and particularly to the end of it, when He was on trial in a certain court-room the night before His death. The presiding official in that court-room was Caiphas, a low type in a high place; the type that finds in religion not a conviction but a career. From an early date his spies had kept him informed concerning Christ, for he had heard strange things concerning the Galilean. Our Lord had driven the buyers and sellers from the Temple, which aroused the ire of the family of the High Priest, for the sons of Annas, the father-in-law of Caiphas, possessed those concessions. Moreover, Our Lord had raised Lazarus from the dead. The miracle exasperated the fellow Sadduces of Caiphas, for they were opposed to the bare idea of a possible resurrection from the dead. It was, therefore, with rather an unholy joy that Caiphas was informed by special messenger that a hurried night trial would bring Jesus before him.

Caiphas entered wearing a long white garment, and wound many times around his waist was a wide purple cincture. Over all he wore a long mantle of dull red color, embroidered with flowers of many hues, and trimmed with gold fringes glistening in the light.

At last Jesus and Caiphas were face to face, and the time for which the High Priest had plotted had really arrived. Imagine the scene in that awful room in the High Priest's house. Since the meeting was illegal, it was probably also informal, but something like the ordinary procedure had to be followed. At the central point of the inner circumference of a semi-circle sat Caiphas, the president of the court; at right and left were seated his colleagues. At each end was a clerk, the one to record votes for acquittal, the other to record votes for conviction. Some of the members that night were sure to have been only half awake, but Caiphas was thoroughly alert. And what a contrast was there between Christ and Caiphas: in the one, insistent good-will to mankind; in the other, cold, contemptuous hate. Suppose that some Alpine climber, in his passion for violent contrasts, carried to the topmost height of some mountain a piece of coal, and suppose when he

137

stood there on the very summit of the virgin peak, isolated and shrouded with the purity of eternal snows, he cast forth the coal. As it lay, black and repellent against the awful purity of the summit, he would see something of that contrast between Caiphas and Christ.

No charge of condemnation could be brought against Christ as long as contradictory statements were made. As soon as one said anything against Him, Sacred Scripture tells us, another contradicted, and a great tumult broke out. One can imagine the charges: One said, "He calls Himself a King," and another contradicted, "No, He does not say that. He only allows others to call Him a King." Another shouted out, "No, as soon as they wanted to proclaim Him a King, He fled away." Some said that He had cured them, but others testified that disease broke out after the cure, and therefore, His cure was done by magic. Some said that Jesus and His Apostles did not offer sacrifice in the temple, while others replied that it was not so. Some tried to prove that Christ and His followers did not celebrate the Passover, but witnesses who were in the Cenacle and had helped to prepare it the day before, denied this. Some said He was an illegitimate Son, but the old priests of the temple contradicted this, saying that His Mother was a pious virgin who passed her youth in the temple. One of the Evangelists records in detail the charge: "This Man said, 'I will destroy this temple made with hands, and within three days I will build another not made with hands.'" But another contradicted him, saying, "No, He did not say that: He said He would build a new temple." And so the disputes went on. The contradictions caused great commotion. Nothing that was said could give any color of justice to the sentence of death. When order was restored, Caiphas, infuriated by the way matters were going, rose up from the divan and came forward to the very edge of the dais. If witnesses had failed to condemn, Christ Himself must furnish the grounds for condemnation. So, turning to the Prisoner, the false-hearted judge addressed Him: "Answerest Thou nothing to the things which these witness against Thee?" But Jesus held His peace.

These silences of Jesus were weighty with magnetic eloquence. He did not speak, but looked with His great calm eyes at the troubled

139

and convulsed faces of His assassins, and, for all eternity, judged those phantom judges. In a flash every one of them was weighed and condemned by that look which went straight to their souls. The cheeks of the ironical old man became red with anger at the silence.

"Well, if He will not speak, then He must be forced to speak and voice His own destruction." Caiphas rose from the seat at the head of the assembly, and, with all the authority that could be crowded into words, asked a question that really mattered, a question that did not center about human affairs, a question which called for an answer as no other question ever asked since the beginning called for an answer, a question that required not one of those vacuous, meaningless answers of timid politicians, but an answer clear-cut like chiseled marble, and the question rang out through the assembly: "I adjure Thee by the Living God, that Thou tell us if Thou be the Christ, the Son of God." Priests and rabbis, Scribes and Pharisees, learned men of Israel, knew what the question meant. "Art Thou the God, foretold by prophets, Who would come to this world as God the Saviour?" Every one sprang to his

140

feet, clawing fingers stretching out toward Him.

Jesus hesitated a moment before dazzling those bleared eyes with the splendor of His formidable secret. A terrible ominous silence settled over the hall that was made the more intense by its contrast with the sound of the distant crowing of a cock. Then came the answer: "Thou hast said it. Nevertheless, I say to you, hereafter you shall see the Son of man sitting on the right hand of the power of God, and coming in the clouds of heaven."

He had given a categorical, straight-forward answer about His Divinity; He defined Himself; He did not say it made any difference if you did not believe; He enunciated a truth, a cold truth, an authoritative principle. *He enunciated a dogma!*

A gleam of satisfaction lighted up the face of Caiphas. He almost sighed a sigh of relief. At last! At last! he had triumphed! His breast was heaving high with the joy of victory. In the shrill voice of an old man, he shouted out: "He hath blasphemed; what further need have we of witnesses?" Drawing out a small knife from under his girdle, and pretending a

141

shocked horror which he did not feel at all, he rent his priestly garments, tore them top to bottom, letting the torn pieces hang like glorious symbols of a victorious battle. Then member after member of the Sanhedrin rent his garments, and the cloaked ghosts felt themselves relieved of an immense weight. "Behold, now you have heard the blasphemy, what think you?" And all in the noisy kennel bayed out their answer: "He is guilty of death." Guilty of death——! Yes, He was too dogmatic.

Now let us suppose that, in answer to that question of Caiphas about His divinity and His divine Sonship, Our Blessed Lord had said: "Far be it from Me, Caiphas, to impose any dogmas concerning my Divinity either upon you or upon posterity. I do not wish to cramp your spiritual freedom by harnessing you with the dogma that I am the Son of God. Religion must be free from dogmas, and the religious experience of each individual must decide whether I am a God or just a mere man." If He had made such a statement, do you think He would have been condemned by Caiphas? If He had been what the modern world calls broad-minded, do you think Caiphas would ever have delivered Him over to Pilate? If He had been less dogmatic, do you think He ever would have been condemned? If He had not been so dogmatic about His divinity, He never would have seen the cross.

Before the unbelieving world rends its garments in holy horror of dogmas, let it pause for a moment to hear the reasoned answer of the Church to the charge of dogmatism. First of all, in direct contradiction of many a modern preachment, the Church holds that it is impossible to have a religion without dogmas. To say that one must have a religion without a dogma is to assert a dogma, and a dogma that needs tremendously more justification than any dogma of the Church. What is a dogma? A dogma is an idea, and in this sense a man without a dogma may be said to be a man without an idea. Dogmas there must be, just as long as there is sound thinking.

History, mathematics, geography, and science all have their dogmas, their abstract principles, and their ideas. That the World War ended on Armistice Day, 1918, is a dogma of history; that Albany is the capital of the State of New York is a dogma of geog-

143

raphy; that the sum of the angles of a triangle is equal to two right angles is a dogma of geometry; that water is made up of two atoms of hydrogen and one of oxygen is a dogma of science. These are luminous truths, sound ideas in various fields of knowledge. Now truths like these in the religious field are called dogmas in the strict sense of the term. That there are Three Persons in One God, that Christ is the Son of God, that faith is a gift, that grace is a participation in the Nature of God, that the Church is the continuation of the Incarnation—these are dogmas of religion.

Now to ask that religion be free from dogmas is like asking that a body be freed from its backbone, or that art be freed from shape and proportion, and that literature be freed from grammar. I know there are thousands of minds weak enough to succumb to the succulent abstraction of the sweet catchword: "I believe in religion, but not in theology," but it is only a catchword. Such a mind might just as well say, "I believe in chemicals, but not in chemistry," or, "I believe in health, but not in all the medical dogmas about digestion, vitamins, and assimilation." It is all as vain and as

144

senseless as saying, "I want to be really scientific, but let us do away with laboratories and technique." An open mind is good—but if it's open all around. . . . Well!

The only difference between the dogmas of religion and the dogmas of science is that the latter are grounded upon the authority of fallible men, while the dogmas of the Church are grounded upon the authority of God revealing. The religious problem is not whether religion shall be free from dogmas or not, because, by the mere fact that a man thinks, he creates dogmas. The real problem is which dogmas are we going to accept, those of hearsay, private wish, or the funded intelligence of an august line of philosophers, saints, and mystics. For the life of me, I cannot see why any one should accept the authority of the Book of Darwin, and not accept the authority of the Book of Isaias; nor how any one can accept the authority of the latest psychological theory emanating from Vienna, and not accept the authority of twenty centuries of Christian tradition; nor how any one can accept the authority of H. G. Wells, and not accept the authority of Jesus Christ!

It is equally untrue to say that the weaving

145

together of dogmas into a creed throughout the course of the Church's life is a departure from the simplicity of the Gospels and a complexity unbecoming to religion. It is one of the inconsistencies of the modern world that it should constantly insist upon evolution and progress, and then, when it finds progress exemplified in the development of doctrine, or the unfolding of the mustard seed into a great tree, it is scandalized.

The oft-repeated demand that the modern world wants a religion based upon the Sermon on the Mount is founded upon a false dogma that only those words of Our Lord which please the modern world shall be accepted as a basis for religion, while all others which do not please it shall be rejected. And, as a matter of fact, the Sermon on the Mount contains a fearful and wonderful complexity of dogmas such as: the first shall be last, and the last first, and that those who sow in tears shall reap in joy, and that the way to save your life is to lose it. There is probably more of dogma in the Sermon on the Mount than in any other sermon ever preached by Our Lord, such as the dogma of the existence of God, the Providence of God,

146

the existence of the soul, the existence of heaven and hell, the beauty of purity, and above all, the dogma which is opposed to everything the modern world holds dear, namely, those who are really God's children will always be hated, reviled, and persecuted by the world. The Church has never made a distinction between the words of Our Lord, and said, "We will accept these, and reject those." She holds that if Our Lord is worthy of belief in speaking of the birds of the air, He is also worthy of belief in speaking of founding His Church upon the Rock who is Peter. And the Church does not stop there. With these truths, the Church has done two things. She has remembered them, and a thousand other truths Our Lord gave, and that memory is tradition. Just as a scientist cannot make any progress unless he goes back to the memory of scientific first principles, and uses them as the ground and foundation of other conclusions, so, too, the Church goes back to her intellectual memory, the unbroken tradition of twenty centuries of solid Christian thinking, as the foundation for further thinking and deeper wisdom. But the Church not only remembers the truths of

147

Christ and the Apostles, which is tradition, but she thinks about these truths, and the harder she thinks, the more thoughts she produces, hence, the more dogmas she develops.

For twenty centuries the Church has been doing a tremendous amount of good, solid, hard thinking, and hence has built up dogmas as a man might build a house of brick but founded on a rock, for dogmas are solid things with which a man can build, not like straw, which is religious experience fit only for burning. And the Church is proud of her complex dogmas, one of which clicks with another like the parts of a perfect machine, or, better still, which coalesce one with another like the various organs of the body. Just as every mathematician is proud of the complexities of his science, and the development of arithmetic into geometry and geometry into calculus; just as every physicist is proud of the complexities of his science, and the increased dogmas concerning matter and then atoms, and then protons and electrons; just as every lawyer is proud of the great traditions of law and of the complexities of principles which form a whole, so too the Church is proud of the complexity of her dog-

148

mas and her truths. No one can write out all
the dogmas of science on a postcard. How,
then, can one expect to do it with the knowledge of God? The Church believes that dogmas
are a sign that reason, and not feeling, dominates her life, and in that respect she stands
whole-heartedly against the vice of our modern
world which believes that progress consists in
breaking with the past, in uprooting tradition
and in casting away dogmas. She teaches that
if there is any such thing as progress, it must
necessarily consist of a growth into more and
more definite convictions and into more and
more dogmas, for just as food is the object of
the stomach, so doctrine is the object of the
mind.

The modern man must decide for himself
whether he is going to have a religion with
thought, or a religion without it. He already
knows that thoughtless politics lead to the ruin
of society, and he may begin to suspect that
thoughtless religion ends in confusion worse
confounded. The problem is simple. The modern man has two maps before him: one the
map of sentimental religion, the other the map
of dogmatic religion. The first is very simple.

It has been constructed only in the last few years by a topographer who has just gone into the business of map-making, and is extremely adverse to explicit directions. He believes that each man should find his own way and not have his liberty taken away by dogmatic directions. The other map is much more complicated and full of dogmatic detail. It has been made by topographers that have been over every inch of the road for centuries and know each detour and each pitfall. It has explicit directions and dogmas such as, "Do not take this road—it is swampy," or "Follow this road; although rough and rocky at first, it leads to a smooth road on a mountaintop." The simple map is very easy to read, but those who are guided by it are generally lost in a swamp of mushy sentimentalism. The other map takes a little more scrutiny, but it is more simple in the end, for it takes you up through the rocky road of the world's scorn to the everlasting hills where is seated the Original Map-Maker, the only One who ever has associated rest with learning: "Learn of Me . . . and you shall find rest for your souls."

Every new coherent doctrine and dogma

adds to the pabulum for thought; it is an extra bit of garden upon which we can intellectually browse; it is new food into which we can put our teeth and thence absorb nourishment; it is the discovery of a new intellectual planet which adds fullness and spaciousness to our mental world. And simply because it is solid and weighty, because it is dogmatic and not gaseous and foggy like a sentiment, it is intellectually invigorating, for it is with weights that the best drill is done, and not with feathers.

It is the very nature of a man to generate children of his brain in the shape of thoughts, and as he piles up thought on thought, truth on truth, doctrine on doctrine, conviction on conviction, and dogma on dogma, in a very coherent and orderly fashion, so as to produce a system complex as a body and yet one and harmonious, the more and more human he becomes. When, however, in response to false cries for progress, he lops off dogmas, breaks with the memory of his forefathers, denies intellectual parentage, pleads for a religion without dogmas, substitutes mistiness for mystery, mistakes sentiment for sediment, he is sinking back slowly, surely, and inevitably into

151

the senselessness of stones and into the irresponsible unconsciousness of weeds. Grass is broadminded. Cabbages have heads—but no dogmas.

THE CURSE OF BROADMINDEDNESS

THE CURSE OF BROADMINDEDNESS

"THE Catholic Church intolerant." That simple thought, like a yellow-fever sign, is supposed to be the one solid reason which should frighten away any one who might be contemplating knocking at the portals of the Church for entrance, or for a crumb of the Bread of Life. When proof for this statement is asked, it is retorted that the Church is intolerant because of its self-complacency and smug satisfaction as the unique interpreter of the thoughts of Christ. Its narrow-mindedness is supposed to be revealed in its unwillingness to coöperate effectively with other Christian bodies that are working for the union of churches. Within the last ten years, two great world conferences on religion have been held, in which every great religion except the Catholic participated. The Catholic Church was invited to attend and discuss the two important subjects of doctrine and ministry, but she refused the invitation.

155

That is not all. Even in our own country she has refused to lend a helping hand in the federating of those churches which decided it was better to throw dogmatic differences into the background, in order to serve better the religious needs of America. The other churches would give her a royal welcome, but she will not come. She will not coöperate! She will not conform! And she will not conform because she is too narrow-minded and intolerant! Christ would not have acted that way!

Such is, practically every one will admit, a fair statement of the attitude the modern world bears to the Church. The charge of intolerance is not new. It was once directed against Our Blessed Lord Himself.

Immediately after His betrayal, Our Blessed Lord was summoned before a religious body for the first Church Conference of Christian times, held not in the city of Lausanne or Stockholm, but in the city of Jerusalem. The meeting was presided over by one Annas, the primate and head of one of the most aggressive families of the patriarchate, a man wise with the deluding wisdom of three score and ten years, in a country in which age and wisdom were synonymous. Five of his sons in succession wore the sacred ephod of blue and purple and scarlet, the symbols of family power. As head of his own house, Annas had charge of family revenues, and from non-biblical sources we learn that part of the family fortune was invested in trades connected with the Temple. The stalls for the sale of bird and beast and material for sacrifice were known as the booths of the sons of Annas. One expects a high tone when a priest goes into business; but Annas was a Sadducee, and since he did not believe in a future life, he made the most of life while he had it. There was always one incident he remembered about his Temple business, and that was the day Our Lord flung his tables down its front steps as if they were lumber, and with cords banished the money-handlers from the Temple like rubbish before the wind.

That incident flashed before his mind now, when he saw standing before him the Woodworker of Nazareth. The eyes of Jesus and Annas met, and the first world conference on religion opened. Annas, ironically feigning surprise at the sight of the prisoner whom multitudes followed the week before, opened the meeting by asking Jesus to make plain two important religious matters, the two that were discussed later on in Lausanne and Geneva and Stockholm, namely, the question of His doctrine and the question of His ministry. Our Lord was asked by a religious man, a religious leader, and a religious authority, representative of the Common faith of a nation, to enter into discussion, to sit down to a conference on the all-important questions of religion—ministry and discipline—and He refused! And the world's first Church Conference was a failure.

He refused in words which left no doubt in the mind of Annas that the doctrine which He preached was the one which He would now uphold in religious conference, namely, His Divinity. With words, cut like the facets of a diamond, and sentences, as uncompromising as a two-edged sword, He answered Annas: "I have spoken openly to the world . . . and in secret spoke I nothing. Why asketh thou Me? Ask them that have heard Me, what I spoke unto them: behold, these know the things which I said."

In so many words Jesus said to Annas: "You imply by your questioning that I am not

158

Divine; that I am just the same as the other rabbis going up and down the country-side; that I am another one of Israel's prophets, and at the most, only a man. I know that you would welcome Me to your heart if I would say that I am only human. But no! I have spoken openly to the world. I have declared My Divinity; I say unto you, I have exercised the right of Divinity, for I have forgiven sins; I have left my Body and Blood for posterity, and rather than deny its reality I have lost those who followed Me, who were scandalized at My words. It was only last night that I told Philip that the Father and I are One, and that I will ask My Father to send the Spirit of Truth to the Church I have founded on Peter, which will endure to the end of time. Ask those who have heard Me; they will tell you what things I have said. I have no other doctrine than that which I declared when I drove your dove-hucksters out of the Temple, and declared it to be My Father's House; that which I have preached; that which angels declared at My birth; that which I revealed on Thabor; that which I now declare before you, namely, My Divinity. And if your first principle is that I

159

am not Divine, but am just human like your-
self, then there is nothing in common between
us. So, why asketh thou Me to discuss doctrine
and ministry with you?"

And some brute standing near by, feeling
himself the humiliation of the high priest at
such an uncompromising response, struck Our
Blessed Lord across the face with a mailed fist,
drawing out of Him two things: blood, and a
soft answer: "If I have spoken evil bear witness of the evil: but if well, why smitest thou
Me?" And that soldier in the court-room of
Annas has gone down in history as the representative of that great group that bears a
hatred against Divinity, the group that never
clothes that hatred in any intellectual language, but rather in violence alone.

All that happened in the life of Christ happens in the life of the Church. And here in the
court-room of Annas I find the reason for the
Catholic Church's refusal to take part in move-
ments for federation such as those inspired by
present world conferences on religion. Happy
the Church is that there should be a desire for
the union of Christendom, but she cannot take
part in any such conference. In so many words

the Church says to those who invited her: "Why askest thou me about my doctrine and my ministry? Ask them that have heard me. I have spoken openly through the centuries, declaring myself the Spouse of Christ, founded on the Rock of Peter. Centuries before prophets of modern religions arose, I spoke my Divinity at Nicea and Constantinople; I spoke it in the cathedrals of the Middle Ages; I speak it to-day in every pulpit and church throughout the world. I know that you will welcome me to your conferences if I say I am not Divine; I know Ritualists throughout the world feel the need of my ceremonials, and would grasp my hand if I would but relinquish my claim to be Divine; I know a recent writer has argued that the great organization of the Church could be the framework for the union of all Christendom, if I would give up my claim to be the Truth; I know the church doors of the world would rejoice to see me pass in; I know your welcome would be sincere; I know you desire the union of all Christendom—but I cannot. 'Why do you ask me?' if your first principle is that I am not Divine, but just a human organization like your own, that I am a human insti-

161

tution like all other human institutions
founded by erring men and erring women. If
your first principle is that I am human, but not
divine, then there is no common ground for
conference. I must refuse."

Call this intolerance, yes! That is just what
it is—the intolerance of Divinity. It is the
claim to uniqueness that brought the blow of
the soldier against Christ, and it is the claim
to uniqueness that brings the blow of the
world's disapproval against the Church. It is
well to remember that there was one thing in
the life of Christ that brought His death, and
that was the intolerance of His claim to be Divine. He was tolerant about where He slept
and what He ate; He was tolerant about short-
comings of His fish-smelling apostles; He was
tolerant of those who nailed Him to the Cross,
but He was absolutely intolerant about His
claim to be Divine. There was not much tolerance about His statement that those who believe not in Him shall be condemned. There was
not much tolerance about His statement that
any one who would prefer his own father or
mother to Him was not worthy of being His

162

disciple. There was not much tolerance of the world's opinion in giving His blessing to those whom the world would hate and revile. Tolerance to His Mind was not always good, nor was intolerance always evil.

There is no other subject on which the average mind is so much confused as the subject of tolerance and intolerance. Tolerance is always supposed to be desirable because it is taken to be synonymous with broadmindedness. Intolerance is always supposed to be undesirable, because it is taken to be synonymous with narrow-mindedness. This is not true, for tolerance and intolerance apply to two totally different things. *Tolerance applies only to persons, but never to principles. Intolerance applies only to principles, but never to persons.* We must be tolerant to persons because they are human; we must be intolerant about principles because they are divine. We must be tolerant to the erring, because ignorance may have led them astray; but we must be intolerant to the error, because Truth is not our making, but God's. And hence the Church in her history, due reparation made, has always welcomed the heretic back into the treasury of her souls, but never his heresy into the treasury of her wisdom.

The Church, like Our Blessed Lord, advocates charity to all persons who disagree with her by word or by violence. Even those who—in the strictest sense of the term—are bigots, are to be treated with the utmost kindness. They really do not hate the Church, they hate only what they mistakenly believe to be the Church. If I believed all the lies that are told about the Church, if I gave credence to all the foul stories told about her priesthood and Papacy, if I had been brought up on falsehoods about her teachings and her sacraments, I would probably hate the Church a thousand times more than they do.

Keeping the distinction well in mind between persons and principles, cast a hurried glance over the general religious conditions of our country. America, it is commonly said, is suffering from intolerance. While there is much want of charity to our fellow-citizens, I believe it is truer to say that America is not suffering so much from intolerance as it is suffering from a false kind of tolerance: the

164

tolerance of right and wrong; truth and error; virtue and vice; Christ and chaos. The man, in our country, who can make up his mind and hold to certain truths with all the fervor of his soul, is called narrow-minded, whereas the man who cannot make up his mind is called broadminded. And now this false broad-mindedness or tolerance of truth and error has carried many minds so far that they say one religion is just as good as another, or that because one contradicts another, therefore, there is no such thing as religion. This is just like concluding that because, in the days of Columbus, some said the world was round and others said it was flat, therefore, there is no world at all.

Such indifference to the oneness of truth is at the root of all the assumptions so current in present-day thinking that religion is an open question, like the tariff, whereas science is a closed question, like the multiplication table. It is behind that queer kind of broadminded-ness which teaches that any one may tell us about God, though it would never admit that any one but a scientist should tell us about an atom. It has inspired the idea that we should

165

be broad enough to publish our sins to any psychoanalyst living in a glass house, but never so narrow as to tell them to a priest in a confessional box. It has created the general impression that any individual opinion about religion is right, and it has disposed modern minds to accept its religion dished up in the form of articles entitled: "My Idea of Religion," written by any nondescript from a Hollywood movie star to the chief cook of the Ritz-Carlton.

This kind of broadmindedness which sacrifices principles to whims, dissolves entities into environment, and reduces truth to opinion, is an unmistakable sign of the decay of the logical faculty.

Certainly it should be reasonably expected that religion should have its authoritative spokesmen, just as well as science. If you had wounded the palm of your hand, you would not call in a florist; if you broke the spring of your watch, you would not ask an artesian-well expert to repair it; if your child had swallowed a nickel, you would not call in a collector of internal revenue; if you wished to determine the authenticity of an alleged Rembrandt, you would not summon a house painter. If you insist that only a plumber should mend the leaks in your pipes, and not an organ tuner, if you demand a doctor shall take care of your body, and not a musician, then why, in heaven's name, should not we demand that a man who tells about God and religion at least say his prayers?

The remedy for this broadmindedness is intolerance, not intolerance of persons, for of them we must be tolerant regardless of views they may hold, but intolerance of principles. A bridge builder must be intolerant about the foundations of his bridge; the gardener must be intolerant about weeds in his gardens; the property owner must be intolerant about his claims to property; the soldier must be intolerant about his country, as against that of the enemy, and he who is broadminded on the battlefield is a coward and a traitor. The doctor must be intolerant about disease in his patients, and the professor must be intolerant about error in his pupils. So, too, the Church, founded on the Intolerance of Divinity, must be equally intolerant about the truths commissioned to her. There are to be no one-fisted battles, no half-drawn swords, no divided loves, no equalizing Christ and Buddha in a broad sweep of sophomoric tolerance or broadmindedness, for as Our Blessed Lord has put it: "He that is not with Me is against Me."

There is only one answer to the problem of the constituents of water, namely, two atoms of hydrogen and one of oxygen. There is only one answer to the question of what is the capital of the United States. There is only one true answer to the problem of two and two. Suppose that certain mathematicians in various parts of this country taught diverse kinds of multiplication tables. One taught that two times two equaled five, another two times two equaled six, another two times two equaled seven and one fourth, another two times two equaled nine and four fifths. Then suppose that some one decided it would be better to be broadminded and to work together and sacrifice their particular solutions for the sake of economy. The result would be a Federation of Mathematicians, compromising, possibly, on the pooled solution that two times two equaled five and seven eighths. Outside this federation

168

is another group which holds that two times two equals four. They refuse to enter the federation unless the mathematicians agree to accept this as the true and unique solution. The broadminded group in conference taunts them, saying: "You are too intolerant and narrow-minded. You smack of the dead past. They believed that in the dark ages."

Now this is precisely the attitude of the Church on the subject of the world conferences on religion. She holds that just as the truth is one in geography, in chemistry, and mathematics, so too there is one truth in religion, and if we are intolerant about the truth that two times two equals four, then we should also be intolerant about those principles on which is hinged the only really important thing in the world, namely, the salvation of our immortal soul. If the assumption is that there is no Divinity, no oneness about truth, but only opinion, probability, and compromise, then the Church must refrain from participation. Any conference on religion, therefore, which starts with the assumption that there is no such thing as truth, and that contrary and contradictory sects may be united in a federation of broad-mindedness, must never expect the Church to join or coöperate.

As we grew from childhood to adolescence, the one thing that probably did most to wreck our faith in Santa Claus—I know it did mine —was to find a Santa Claus in every department-store window. If there were only one Santa Claus, and he was at the North Pole, how could there be one in every shop window and at every street corner? That same mentality which led us to seek truth in unity should lead us in religious matters to identically the same conclusion.

The world may charge the Church with intolerance, and the world is right. The Church is intolerant—intolerant about Truth, intolerant about principles, intolerant about Divinity, just as Our Blessed Lord was intolerant about His Divinity. The other religions may change their principles, and they do change them, because their principles are man-made. The Church cannot change, because her principles are God-made. Religion is not a sum of beliefs that we would like, but the sum of beliefs God has given. The world may disagree

170

with the Church, but the world knows very definitely with what it is disagreeing. In the future as in the past, the Church will be intolerant about the sanctity of marriage, for what God has joined together no man shall put asunder; she will be intolerant about her creed, and be ready to die for it, for she fears not those who kill the body, but rather those who have the power to cast body and soul into hell. She will be intolerant about her infallibility, for "Lo," says Christ, "I am with you all the days even unto the end of the world." And while she is intolerant even to blood, in adhering to the truths given her by her Divine Founder, she will be tolerant to those who say she is intolerant, for the same Divine Founder has taught her to say: "Father, forgive them, they know not what they do."

There are only two positions to take concerning truth, and both of them had their hearing centuries ago in the court-room of Solomon where two women claimed a babe. A babe is like truth; it is one; it is whole; it is organic and it cannot be divided. The real mother of the babe would accept no compromise. She was intolerant about her claim. She must have the

171

whole babe, or nothing—the intolerance of Motherhood. But the false mother was tolerant. She was willing to compromise. She was willing to divide the babe—and the babe would have met its death through broadmindedness.

PATRIOTISM——TRUE AND FALSE

ONE issue which will always hold interest is
the conflict between Church and State. If one
were to set down in some order the objections
against the Church on the part of the modern
State, these objections might resolve themselves into these three: first, the Church is perverting the nation not only by having a paro-
chial school system which embodies a different
educational policy from that of the public
school, but also by her marriage legislation
which admits of no divorce—now the generally accepted thing in society; secondly, the
Church refuses to give tribute to America, in
as much as her heart is across the sea, recog-
nizing the Vicar of Christ supreme in matters
spiritual, and also because her heart is too
much interested in the next world, and not
sufficiently devoted to this one; thirdly, the
Church looks upon herself as a sort of King in
the sense that she claims to be the unique
Church of Christ, and refuses absolutely to ac-

cept the democratic principle that one religion is just as good as another. Such are, I believe, the three principal complaints and charges against the Church to-day, and to those who urge them I would remind that they are exactly the same charges that were directed against Our Blessed Lord Himself in His trial before Pilate.

Since the year 26, Pontius Pilate had been procurator in the name of Tiberius Cæsar. Little was known of him before that time. He had been in Judea only a few years, but long enough to draw upon himself the bitterest hate of those over whom he ruled. Sometime before the trial, Pilate had come from Caesarea to Jerusalem to take up winter quarters, bringing with him not only effigies of Cæsar on the army banners, but even images of Roman eagles which he introduced in the Temple, without the knowledge of the Jewish people, when the city was asleep. They asked Pilate to remove them, but he would not for fear of injuring Cæsar. For five days and nights they stormed about him, and on the sixth day he erected a judgment seat in the open city behind which he concealed his soldiers. The mo-

ment they repeated their request, Pilate told
them they would all be killed if they did not
leave off disturbing him. But they threw themselves on the ground and laid their necks bare
and said they would rather taste death than
transgress the wisdom of their fathers. Pilate,
deeply affected, ordered the images removed.

The Jews hated Pilate. They did not forget
this incident nor that time when he introduced
votive tablets to the Emperor in Herod's palace in Jerusalem, nor when he confiscated the
money of the Temple to provide luxurious
baths such as he had in Rome and put down a
revolt against his authority with naked swords
and enjoyed his ablutions and Jewish money
in comparative peace.

That Friday at dawn, Pontius Pilate,
wrapped in toga, still sleepy and yawning, was
waiting for a mob in Herod's palace, very ill
disposed toward the trouble makers who forced
him to rise at such an early hour. The crowd of
accusers and the rough populace finally came
to the front of the palace, but they stopped
outside. Why? Because before Pilate's judgment seat, on the paved stones of the Litho-
stratos, was painted a long white line, marking

the boundaries beyond which no Jew could pass without becoming defiled. If they entered the house of a pagan, they were contaminated, and could not eat the Passover. So Caiphas, Annas, and the other accusers stopped at the line. The hypocrites! They were not afraid of innocent blood, but they were afraid of a white line.

Pilate went to that line and asked abruptly: "What accusation bring you against this man?" The Jews knew very well they could not win Pilate's favor if they charged the Christ with attacks upon the religion of their fathers. They were, therefore, ready to lie. Those who are bent upon evil look upon an accessory infamy as of little consequence. Pilate, they knew, could be conquered only by appealing to his loyalty to Rome and to the Emperor. They would give a political coloring to the accusation. If they told him what they told Annas and Caiphas, that Christ was a false Messiah, Pilate would sneer; but if they said He was a seditious inciter of revolt, that He was stirring up the people against the government, that He was unpatriotic, that He was inimical to the best interests of their country, Pilate

178

could do no less than put Him to death. In other words, the charge of blasphemy is abandoned as soon as they enter the prætorium, and the charge of sedition is taken up. The judgment against Our Lord shifts now from religious grounds, where it had been laid before Annas and Caiphas, to patriotic grounds before Pilate. Note the irony of it all!

These same people who had risen against Pilate's authority, who hated him as a Roman, as a symbol of foreign domination and their own slavery, who hated him still more as Pontius Pilate, as plotter against their religion, and thief of their money—these very people now drown their hate, protest their loyalty to Cæsar, their affection for his security, their readiness to accept no Cæsar but him because they found a new hate, a new enemy of their bitter hearts—Christ Jesus Our Lord.

And up against the marble balustrade of Pilate's judgment seat, the charges rolled, and they were three:

1. "We have found this man perverting our nation;

2. Forbidding to give tribute to Cæsar;

3. Saying He is Christ, the King."

The same charges brought against the Church to-day! Every word was lie! He was not perverting the nation; He was bringing balm to wounded hearts and healing to palsied limbs; He was making of that unhappy and degraded people a blessed kingdom of saints. "I am come that they may have life and may have it more abundantly. Come to Me, all you that labor, and are burdened, and I will refresh you." He was not refusing to give tribute to Cæsar. Had not the Scribes and the Pharisees already been convinced this was not true when they asked: "Is it lawful to give tribute to Cæsar?" and heard in answer the divine reply: "Render to Cæsar the things that are Cæsar's and to God the things that are God's." He was not attempting to make Himself King, for one day when the people would have taken Him by force and made Him King, he fled away into the mountain alone. Pilate did not take much notice of the first two charges for he well knew that his enemies could not suddenly become zealots of Cæsar.

Pilate sought to release Our Lord by appealing to the patriotism of the Jews. At that time there was languishing in prison a political assassin by the name of Bar Rabban, who, because of hatred of Judea's pagan masters and a zealot among the Jews and a "patriot" even unto the shedding of blood for the Jewish cause, had made trouble for the Roman government. This "patriot" martyr, persecuted by foreigners, is trotted alongside Our Lord before the great judgment throne of Pilate. Pilate was sure there could be no doubt of their choice. He would give them a patriot if they loved patriotism, and a patriot of the Jews, not of the Romans.

And so Pilate brought out before the mob Christ and Barabbas, virtue and vice, innocence and guilt, purity and foulness, God and man, and the mob was asked to choose between the two. "Whom will you that I release to you, Barabbas, or Jesus that is called Christ?" "Release unto us Barabbas!" rent the air. "But what shall I do with your King?" "Crucify Him! Crucify Him! We love no king but Cæsar!" They might have added: "We are one hundred per cent Romans!"

Pilate wore a worried look. A liveried slave brought him a basin and ewer and began to pour water on his unsteady hands. Pilate held them up dripping in the morning light. They were white, delicate hands, and the jewels on his fingers answered gaily to the sun: "I am innocent of the blood of this just Man. Look you to it." But Pilate's hands are still blood-stained and will be for all eternity—all the waters of the seven seas would not have been enough to wash the blood incarnadine from his hands. He was weak, afraid of a small group though he was Pilate, and history still says in its creed: "He suffered under Pontius Pilate."

In this trial before Pilate there is unfolded the whole history of the Church in relation to the world. The charges brought against Our Lord—all false—are the same charges brought against the Church to-day. And what is particularly striking about them all is that patriotism is made the cloak for them all. There is nothing so sublime that cannot be prostituted, and even the noble virtue of patriotism may have its prostitutors. Samuel Johnson once truly said that "patriotism is the last refuge of the scoundrel," and how true, for just as many sins are committed in its name as in the name of liberty.

As the accusers of Our Blessed Lord covered
182

themselves with the assumed virtue of patriotism, so do the enemies of the Church, and their charges are just as untrue and unwarranted as the charges directed against Our Blessed Lord Himself. First, the Church is not perverting the nation. If our nation has any ideal at all it certainly has the ideal of stability, which means that it must resolve to survive and to march steadily onward in the vanguard of civilization. Now I ask you what forces are best suited to give to our government this very desirable stability? Will the forces of birth-control which limit the number of our citizens by refusing to bring into the world the very units of democratic social life make for its stability? Will the loose divorce laws of our country, which break up families, the very core of national life, make for its endurance? Will the loose morality, which believes that anything is right providing one is not caught, make for a strong and disciplined and stable nation? These are the forces which are decaying and breaking down our national life. But the only single force in America to-day which opposes these destructive elements is the spiritual force of the Church. By what logic, then, can the Church be said to be perverting the nation? If in centuries to come there are eyes to look upon the flag and there are lungs to breathe the air of freedom and there are hearts to respond to America's anthem, it will be because there is a divine power operating in American life, teaching that marriage is a sacred thing and that the children of to-day are the citizens of to-morrow. Break up husband and wife, and you break the family; break the family and you break the children; break them, and you wreck a nation. That is just what the Church is trying to avert, and in doing so, instead of perverting the nation, the Church is making it stable enough to endure, that in centuries to come it may draw down upon itself the blessings of a pleased and Almighty Father.

Secondly, the Church is not refusing to give full tribute to America. Because her spiritual head is in Rome it no more follows that she loves her country less than does any citizen of this land whose mother is in the green isle of Ireland. The Church and the State belong to two distinct spheres and there may be, therefore, a true and loyal allegiance to both, for we

184

are to "render unto Cæsar the things that are Cæsar's, and to God the things that are God's." As a matter of fact, only those who love the spiritual can ever love the natural. Full and loving service of the Church of Christ no more conflicts with the love of nation, than the love of the soul is at variance with the love of the body. The loves, paradoxical though they may seem, merge into unity, thanks to the charity of our Sovereign Head who loved his own country even to the point of weeping over its capital city, and shedding the salt tears of the first Christian Patriot. He who reserved the first fruits of His message for the lost sheep of Israel was the same One whose flame of charity embraced the whole world, and whose life was surrendered on the gibbet of a Cross for the redemption of all people, for all climes and all times.

St. Francis Assisi loved his own country to the passionate degree that on dying he asked to be carried to a hill to see and bless for the last time his beloved country-side, and yet, that love of nationalism no way prevented that soul of his from embracing not only man, but the beasts and birds, not only the fires and the

185

forests, but above all, the Spiritual Father of Christendom who gave him the right to found an order which to-day lights the torches of its charity at the fiery heart of that same poor man of Assisi. St. Paul, too, who loved his own country, was proud of being of the race of Abraham, a Hebrew and a son of a Hebrew, but the love for his own people in no way conflicted with those wider interests where there are no distinctions between Jew and Greek, barbarian or freeman—where there is nothing but the consuming love to be dissolved and to be with Christ.

And what is true of Francis and Paul is true of each loyal son of the Church. We Catholics will give way to no one in the depth of our allegiance to America, and in our allegiance to America we will give way to no one in our allegiance to Christ.

Finally, it is not true that the Church is calling herself a King, and is flying in the face of the democratic principle of equality. What is the foundation of equality? Do those doctrines which hold that one fifth of the population of this country, the Catholic population, is unpatriotic, make for true patriotism of

186

equality? Will the jingoism of the superiority of the Nordic over the Latin make for true equality? Will the mere lip worship of the brotherhood of man on the singing of a common anthem reduce men to unity? The fact is, men do not naturally love men. Beauty is a stronger attraction than the mere cry of equality and fraternity. Where find, then, the real force behind equality? There is only one foundation for equality, and that is the Catholic doctrine that all men have been redeemed by the precious blood of Jesus Christ, that all men have been called to share His life, and that president and citizen, poor and rich, the mighty and the lowly, have been thought so much worth while that Christ would have died for the least of them; that the beggar in the Bowery and the man in the gilded apartment are equal in the eyes of God. And in order to impress this unity on her people, the Church preaches the doctrine of the Eucharist, in which all communicants partake of the same bread in order that they might have the same life, for eating the one bread they are the one Body. The Church, thus, gives to humanity a new beauty and a new reason for loving all

187

men. There is no power in the world making
for equality amongst men, so capable of drawing them together into holy bonds of peace and
love, so destined to melt all differences of race
and blood as the Communion rail of the Cath-
lic Church, for there equality is based upon
common purity of heart in Christ Jesus Our
Lord.

These charges against the Church have
their root and foundation in what has become
the supreme concern of modern life, namely,
nationalism. When I say nationalism, I do not
mean patriotism, for nationalism is patriotism
without a heart. When I say nationalism, I
do not mean national self-government, for
nationalism is a certain spirit in which self-
government is conducted. Nationalism is the
sacrifice of general unity to local feeling—a
kind of Calvinistic damnation of other nations,
and a deification of our own; in other words, a
hatred and a chauvinism. In its origin it is due
to a decline in the belief in God, for as men
forget the True God, they make new a god for
themselves. The new one they are now falling
down before in adoration is the nation.

Nationalism has become, in its extreme

form, a kind of religion which prompts sacrifice and exalts emotions. It is commonly assumed by its devotees that enthusiasm for it as a god is quite sufficient to preserve it as a nation. As a matter of fact, no such enthusiasm will ever save a nation. "Unless the Lord build the house, they labor in vain that build it." The very moment that Edith Cavell, the patron saint of patriotism, was shot through with the great white shaft of death, she cried out as one discovering a tremendous secret: "I see now that patriotism is not enough."

Americans must realize that those things which make a millionaire do not necessarily make a man; that a nation is not great because of the abundance of the things it possesses any more than Dives was greater than Lazarus; that great wealth does not make a great nation, for greatness would then be in what it has rather than in what it does; that great armies and navies, long-range guns and flying-boats do not make a nation great any more than physical prowess made Goliath greater than David; that international budgets, gold reserves, do not make a nation great any more than it made the Queen of Sheba greater than

Solomon: "Woe to them that go down to Egypt for help, trusting in horses . . . because they are many, and in horsemen, because they are very strong."

True greatness resides in qualities of the heart, in charity, justice, peace, purity, love; it is the development of our inner life, the enriching of our minds, the strengthening of our wills, the purification of our hearts; and the people who are bearers of the deepest love, the holiest faith, and work most firmly under the inspiration of the Leader on the Cross—these are the true patriots of America! And these are the patriots the Church is striving to produce by reminding man that he reaches his highest point of development when he conquers the forces of nature by his knowledge, and then in turn is conquered by Christ the King, who, in His turn, in His human nature, is subject to His own Heavenly Father, and who will, at the end of time, deliver all things unto Him. True civilization is a recognition of the primacy of the spiritual: "All are yours, you are Christ's and Christ is God's."

The three charges have found popular expression in words uttered not so long ago by the so-called philosopher, Bertrand Russell, who said that a grave danger faces America, for in one hundred and fifty years from now it will be Catholic. I am not so sure that in one hundred and fifty years from now America will be Catholic, but if it is to be Catholic, it will have to do two more things than it is doing now: It will have to begin to think, and it will have to begin to pray.

Just suppose that that prophecy of Bertrand Russell's did come true. Suppose that every one in America were Catholic. Suppose that every citizen to-morrow morning knelt down and said his prayers to God. Suppose that as each citizen went to work—the judge to his bench, the lawyer to his court, the doctor to his patient, the clerk to his office, the employee to his employer, that each and every one of them was convinced that some day they would have to render an account for even the least actions of their daily life, although unseen by men. Suppose that all the children went to a school in which they heard the name of God, and drank in sweet stories about His Mother and the Saints. Suppose that the students who went to the universities learned not vague theories about sex, but the beauty of chastity, bringing the reward of the vision of God. Suppose that all the divorce courts of our land closed, and that at least once every month every man and woman and child would kneel at the Communion-rail and receive into his very soul the very God who died on the Cross for them. Do you think that would be a menace to American life? If that is a menace, then peace is a menace, then justice is a menace, then charity is a menace, then Christ is a curse!

May all such un-Christian sentiments and every unhuman sentiment pass from our midst, and as days roll into weeks, and weeks into years, may one lesson more and more become deeply embedded in the consciousness of our national life, and that lesson is the message of this discourse—that Catholics will never love America because she is great, but America will be great because Catholics love her.

THE UNWORLDLY IN THE WORLD

THE UNWORLDLY IN THE WORLD

ONE of the catchwords which keeps unthinking minds from Truth and Life is that "The Church is behind the times." The "acids of modernity" are supposed to have eaten away traditional morality, and yet the Church clings on to the same beliefs and practices held centuries ago. Not only that, but if we are to believe her critics, the Church never does the worldly thing. The worldly thing to do to-day, according to the modern mind, is to accept divorce and pagan morality as progressive and forward-looking practices, and yet the Church refuses to compromise, in the slightest, her age-old teaching, even if in so doing she would better harmonize with the demands of the twentieth century.

Thousands of people, it is said, would join the Church to-morrow if she would only relax her moral discipline, or readjust her idea of God to suit the new astrophysics, or recognize divorce as the Christian sects have done. But

the Church remains adamant; the world asks
for one thing; and the Church gives it another.
But if she will not change with the world, then
she shall die. Such is the pronouncement of
modern prophets.

As modern as this charge sounds, let us turn
back the scroll of history to see just how an-
cient it is, and we will discover that Herod
condemned Our Blessed Lord on exactly the
same grounds the world to-day condemns the
Church.

Herod was that type which might be char-
acterized as a splendid animal. Descended as
he was from Herod the Great, who murdered
his own wife and slaughtered the children of
Bethlehem, he combined gross sensuality with
an artistic temperament which manifested itself in his fine taste for buildings—which he
was always careful to dedicate to the Emperor.
As Governor of Galilee, living at Tiberias on
the shore of the sea, he often came up to Jerusalem for the great feasts of the Jews, and
stopped at the house of his half-brother Philip.
There he seduced his brother's wife, Herodias,
and her young daughter, Salome, and drove

from his own house, his own legal wife, the daughter of Aretas, King of Arabia.

Sinful life always palls after its brief hour, and Herod was obliged to seek new thrills for his already jaded life. News comes to him that down along the banks of the Jordan, amid the tamarisks and the green trees lining its banks, as its yellow waters sweep through the desert into the Dead Sea, there is a strange and eloquent man who lives on wild locusts, who is clothed in camel's skin, whose name is John the Baptist.

Not because he was interested in John's doctrine, but because, as in the case of so many in our day, religion is interesting only for its emotional life, he summoned the saint, and bade him come unto him.

And John accepted. The court was delighted for they were eager to hear his rugged eloquence, and just for a moment to feel their wearied and wasted systems awakened into new life by the strange and novel sensation of a sermon in the house of gold.

At the appointed hour, the man whom Our Lord had called "the greatest man of woman born" stepped on to the temporary pulpit erected for him in the court. From the worldly point of view, the proper thing for John to have done, on such an occasion, would have been to flatter the vices and excesses of the king. The unworldly and the impolite thing would have been to condemn the adulterous life of the king. John was keener on pleasing God rather than on pleasing man, and stretching out his hand to the throne, and pointing directly to the one sitting there, he thundered out: "It is not lawful for thee to have thy brother's wife"—and before he knew it, chains were about his wrists, and iron bars before his eyes. How differently many a modern preacher would have acted!

The birthday of Herodias soon rolls around, and lest silence which is often an unbearable repartee, should throw him back on his conscience, and perhaps salvation, Herod plans a mighty banquet. Everything that could satisfy a tongue was served. Bronzed slaves ministered to the appetites with all the delicacies of the fishery, the fields and the vineyards. Presently, the tetrarch became full of wine. He gave a signal, and great purple curtains at the other end of the banquet hall parted, where there was disclosed the sparingly clad form of Salome, the daughter of Herodias by her first husband. Accompanied by slow, voluptuous music, the dancing girl whirled to the wild climax of her passionate theme. Herod, who had his eyes sealed upon her, became maddened more by the dance, than by the wine. Before the curtain had time to drop, the tetrarch, giddy with extreme pleasure, sends for the girl, bidding her tell him what love-token she will have from him, swearing to her that if it be half his kingdom, it shall be hers. The child, already schooled by her mother, answers: "Give me here on a dish the head of John the Baptist."

Before the music had completely ceased, a guardsman crossed the threshold of the banquet hall, bearing aloft in a silver charger, the head of John the Baptist.

The vision of that decapitated head haunted Herod, and one day when he heard talk of the miracles of Our Blessed Lord, he said to one of his courtiers: "This is John the

Baptist; he has risen from the dead." From that time on, he kept close watch on Our Lord. One day a Pharisee came to Our Lord and said to him: "Depart and get Thee hence, for Herod hath a mind to kill Thee." Our Lord answered by calling Herod a "fox." Weeks and months pass, and now at Jerusalem, before the murderer of John, and the son of the man who slew the babes at Bethlehem, there stands the One whom John announced: the grown Babe of Bethlehem, now the Man of Nazareth. And Herod was glad. Glad at such a moment? Yes! St. Luke, describing the scene, tells that he was "very glad," for he hoped to see some miracle done by Him.

Herod greets Our Lord as he would have greeted a performer who might enter his court to while away the tedium of an hour. He received the Son of God as a sensational wonder-man, who might amuse a jaded, profligate court, by some startling trick of magic, or by some marvel of jugglery. He wanted the sensational and the new to gratify his curiosity. It was his nerves and not his soul that wanted the thrill. After all, according to Herod, was not the world given for enjoyment of every fleeting moment, and was not the human being born into the world to have a good time, and rob monotony of its victory?

Herod questioned Our Lord, and we can well imagine what some of the questions were: How He escaped the massacre instituted by his father at Bethlehem? Why He called him fox? What was the meaning of His triumphal entry into Jerusalem last Sunday?

But to all the questions Our Lord gave only the answer of His withering silence. He who spoke to sinful Magdalene, and to the woman taken in sin, to little children, to the deceitful Annas, the mean Caiphas, the weak Pilate, now refuses to speak a single word to the one man who could save Him from crucifixion.

From a worldly point of view, Our Lord did the foolish thing. What would you think of a man before a court who might clear himself of a charge by a word, or a show of power, and yet refused to do so? Well, here is Our Lord going to the Cross and to death, simply because He will not do the worldly thing. Herod wanted one thing, and Christ gave him another. Herod wanted a trick—something to relieve the intolerable monotony of his sensuous life. He wanted fireworks, and He who claimed to be the Light of the World, offered him Light instead, the white flame without flicker of a Divine Personality, in the lantern of His sacred Humanity. That was foolishness! The folly of Omnipotence! And so Herod robed Him in the garment of a fool!

And from that day to this, the Church has been robed in the garment of a fool, because she never does the worldly thing. Her saints are fools, because they plunge after poverty like other men dig after gold, tear at their body while other men pamper theirs, and dare even to swing the world a trinket at their wrist, in order that they might gain an everlasting crown. Her devout nuns are fools who leave the lights and glamours of the world, for the shades and shadows of the Cross, where saints are made; her priests are fools because they practise celibacy in a world which has gone crazy about sex. The Vicar, the Pontiff, is a fool, for refusing to relax the doctrine of Christ concerning the sanctity of marriage, when every other Christian sect under the sun has relaxed it. Yes, the Church is a fool, and all her loyal members are fools, but they are

202

fools only from the world's point of view, not from God's point of view, for with the foolish things of the world hath God chosen to confound the wise, and the weak things of the world to confound the strong. The Church must always bear the taunt of being unmodern and unworldly, as Our Lord had to bear it before Herod. And Our Lord warned us that it would be the mark of the Divinity of the Church: "If you had been of the world, the world would love its own: but because you are not of the world, but I have chosen you out of the world, therefore the world hateth you. . . . If the world hate you, know you that it hath hated Me before you." In other words, "if you ever want to discover My religion on the face of the earth, look for the Church that does not get along with the world." The religion that gets on with the world, and is accepted by it, is worldly; the religion that does not get on with the world is other-worldly, which is another way of saying that it is divine.

The Church is very modern, if modern means serving the times in which we live, but she is not modern, if it means believing that whatever is modern is true. The Church is modern, if modern means that her members should change their hats with the seasons, and even with the styles, but she is not modern, if it means that every time a man changes his hat, he should also change his head, or in an applied sense, that she should change her idea of God every time psychology puts on a new shirt, or physics a new coat.

She is modern, if modern means incorporating the new-found wisdom of the present with the patrimony of the centuries, but she is not modern, if it means sneering at the past as one might sneer at a lady's age. She is modern, if modern means a passionate desire to know the truth, but she is not modern if it means that truth changes with the calendar, and that what is true on Friday is false on Saturday. The Church is modern if modern means progress toward a fixed ideal, but she is not modern if it means changing the ideal instead of attaining it.

The Church is like an old schoolmaster— the schoolmaster of the centuries—and as such she has seen so many students pass before her, cultivate the same poses, and fall into the same errors, that she merely smiles at those who believe that they have discovered a new truth; for in her superior wisdom and experience, she knows that many a so-called new truth is only a new label for an old error. Experience has taught her that the Modernism of 1930 is not the Modernism of 1950, and that what one generation believes to be true, the next will believe to be false; and that the surest way to be a widow in the next age is to marry the spirit of the present one. To-day she is accused of being behind the times because she does not go mad about Freud, and I dare say, that in fifty years from now, if one of the teachers in any of our great universities mounted his rostrum and talked Freud, he would be considered just as antiquated and behind the times as a politician who to-day might mount a soap-box at the corner of 42nd and Broadway, and open a campaign for William McKinley as President.

It is about time that the modern world gave up expecting the Church to die because she is "behind the times." Really she is behind the scenes, and knows just when the curtain will fall on each new fad and fancy. If an announcement had been made a thousand times

205

about a death, and the funeral never took
place, men would soon begin to take the funeral as a joke. And so it is with the Church.
She is always supposed to be behind the times,
and yet it is she who lives beyond the times.
At least a hundred men in every century since
her birth have tolled the bells for her funeral,
but the corpse never appeared. They are always buying coffins for her, but it is they who
use the coffins. They are always assisting at
her apparently last breath, and yet she moves.
They are always digging her grave, and it is a
grave into which the diggers fall. The taunt
that she is "behind the times" and "out of
touch with the world," will never annoy her,
for she knows that it is easy to be in the swim,
in the sense of being "up to the times," for
even a dead body can float down stream. It
takes a live body to resist the current. It is easy
to say we should change our morality to suit
the so-called new ideas about sex, just as it was
easy to say a few centuries ago we should be
Calvinists. It is always easy to let the world
have its way; the difficult thing and the noble
thing is to keep God's way. It is easy to fall;
there are a thousand angles at which a thing
206

will fall, but there is only one at which it will stand, and that is the angle at which the Church is posed between heaven and earth, and from that angle she has sung a requiem over all the prophets of the past who ever said that she was dying, and she will continue to sing requiems over the prophets of the future, for the story of her life is the story of John in the court-room of Herod.

Salome danced, and as she danced she kept pace with the time to be the earthly symbol of all those who change to keep up with the times. As she danced two men lost their heads. Herod lost his head figuratively, for he believed that a man should move with the times, and that it was lawful to live with another man's wife; John lost his head literally, for he believed that a man should not change with the times, and that it was not lawful for a man to live with another's wife. The Church believes that John was right and Herod wrong. Being a saint, which is the foolishness which purchases eternity, means losing one's head John's way, rather than Herod's.

THE IGNORANCE OF THE LEARNED

THE IGNORANCE OF THE LEARNED

FOUR judges sat in judgment against the Lord and Saviour of the world, and they condemned Him to death on contradictory charges. He was condemned for being too dogmatic before Caiphas, because He enunciated the doctrine of His Divinity; He was accused of being too undogmatic before Annas, because He refused to make any pronouncements concerning His doctrine and His ministry; He was accused of being too worldly before Pilate because He was perverting the nation; He was accused of being too unworldly before Herod, because He refused to do the worldly thing, and perform a trick of magic to gain His release. Too dogmatic! Too undogmatic! Too worldly! Too unworldly! Men could not agree on why He should die, but they did agree that He should die. Where find a fitting punishment for one condemned on contradictory charges? The only fitting death for one condemned on contradictory charges is not scourging, nor stoning, but the crucifixion, for on the Cross one bar is at variance or contradiction with another.

And so the King went to His death—for a bed, a Cross; for a pillow, a crown of thorns; and lest His hands and feet should slip out, they tucked them in with nails. A King is hanging from a peg—aye, more than a King —Truth, Justice, Mercy, God.

And the three great civilizations of the world saw Him hang, and suffer and die, for He was crucified in the language of Hebrew, Latin, and Greek, in the civilizations of Jerusalem, Rome, and Athens, in the name of religion, law, and morality, in the name of the good, the true, and the beautiful. Jerusalem was the city of religion, and it condemned the One who brought it religion; Latin Rome was the city of law, and it condemned the Lawmaker; Athens was the city of morality, and it condemned the Sinless. Representatives of each of these civilizations passed beneath the banner of the Cross, and hurled the challenge each in their own language, "Come down from the Cross and we will believe." What happened in those terrible moments of hate was not something that would pass into history, as did the battle of Marathon; what was happening was the first scene in an abiding drama, the curtain of which will not ring down until the crack of doom. It is now the Mystic Christ, or the Church, which is hanging on the Cross, and to-day, just as twenty centuries ago, she is being crucified in the modern civilizations of Jerusalem, Rome, and Athens, in the name of modern religion, modern law, and modern morality.

Modern religion marches beneath the Cross, looks up to the Church crucified thereon by an unbelieving world, and who is there who has not heard the marchers say at least a thousand times: "Come down from your belief in infallibility. Come down from your belief in the primacy of Peter. Come down from your attachment to the Divinity of Christ. Come down from your devotion to the Virgin Mary and the Saints. Come down from your belief that you are the one, true, unique spouse, the Church of Christ. Can you not see that there are other crosses on Calvary besides your own? Come down and we will believe!"

And next modern law, modern in the sense that it has broken with Christian tradition,

213

takes it stand beneath the Cross, and who is there who is not already familiar with its taunts and pleadings:"Come down from your belief in the law of eternal justice! Come down from your belief in hell. Come down from your belief that the laws of Christ are more sound than the laws of State! Come down from your belief in the law of mortification, for who is there in the pagan world who wants your penance and your suffering? Look to the sorry end it has brought you now! Come down from your Cross, and we will believe!"

And finally, the third of the enduring civilizations, the teachers of modern morality, advances beneath the same Cross, and who is there living in this great era of carnality who has not heard their taunts a thousand times as they sneer at the Church: "Come down from your belief in the sanctity of marriage! Come down from your belief in virginity and celibacy! Come down from your age-long opposition to divorce. Come down from your opposition to sex, when all the world is mad about it! Come down from your opposition to birth-control! Can you not see that the acids of modernity have eaten away your age-old moral-

214

ity? Come down from the Cross, and we will believe."

But the Church does not come down, though ten thousand times ten thousand tongues are loud in their pleading. It does not come down because Christ did not come down. It is easy to step from great heights when the world scorns, but it is the sign of a martyr to die for an ideal. It is easy to come down and follow the world, but it is nobler to remain suspended and draw the world to oneself. It is human to come down, but it is divine to hang there.

But will there never be a reconciliation between the world and the Church? Must the one always be hanging on the Cross in apparent defeat, and the other walking the earth in apparent victory? Ah, there is the possibility of a reconciliation, and it resides in the words of forgiveness pronounced the first time by Our Blessed Lord on the Cross, and now repeated for the thousandth time by the Church on its Cross.

And what were those words? They were words of a prayer—words that fell in a voice calm and low, heard above the shaking of dice, the moans of dying thieves, the sobs of a Magdalene and the sighs of a Mary—a prayer heard in heaven and earth—a prayer that went out from Calvary's hills and re-echoes to our own ears to-day: "Father forgive them, for they know not what they do."

Forgive whom? Forgive those who crucify in the name of modern religion, modern law, and modern morality, in the language of Hebrew and Latin and Greek? Forgive them? Why? Because they know what they do? No. Because they know *not* what they do! It is only the ignorance of what is involved in their great crime which brings them within the pale of the mercy of the One on the Cross, and the forgiveness of the heavenly Father. It is solely and uniquely because they know not what they do that there is a possibility of forgiveness. There is not redemption for the fallen angels, simply because they knew what they were doing. But we do not always know what we are doing. If we did, and still did it, we would never be saved. It is not wisdom that saves! It is ignorance!

Will Annas be forgiven because he knew the Talmud from beginning to end? Will Caiphas be forgiven because he knew the details of the law of the Sanhedrin? Will Pilate be forgiven because he knew Roman law? Will Herod be forgiven because he knew how to be a tetrarch? Will the followers of modern religion, modern law, and modern morality be forgiven because of what they know? They know something about Einstein's theory and the necessity of a cosmical religion; they know the latest book of the month, and the new morals which have supplanted Christianity; they know all the spurious arguments in favor of birth-control; they know the new psychological theory emanating from Vienna in which the soul is reduced to sex; they know the movement of world politics; they know the world, its ways, its sin, its crime, its fiction; they know all these things and they are proud of what they know, and yet not a single one of them will be saved because of what he knows. They will come within the fold of Divine forgiveness only on condition that they learn to know that they do not know everything. If their learning is going to make them proud of rejecting Christ and the moral laws; if it is going to make them dispense with redemption as a pagan myth, conscience as an illusion, God

217

as an ideal—then they will never be happy, then they will never be saved. Why, they would be damned if it were not for their ignorance of the terrible thing they are doing when they leave God and Christ out of their lives! It is not wisdom that saves—it is ignorance!

Will the executioners be saved because they knew what they did when they unfurled Our Blessed Lord like a wounded eagle upon the banner of salvation? Will the bigots who say all manner of evil things against the Church, her priests, her doctrine, her faithful; will the leaders of Bolshevism who attempt to root out religion from the hearts of people as if it were an opiate; will those who spread venomous lies about the Vicar of Christ; will all those whose love for modern religion, modern law and modern morality, which can find no other expression or outlet except in cries of hate and bitterness; will all those who persecute the Church and thus nail Christ anew to the Cross, be saved because they know what they are doing? It is only because they are ignorant of what the Church really is, that they are brought within hearing of the cry of the Cross. If Saul knew what he was doing in persecuting

the Church of Damascus, when Christ called
out to him from the heavens, he would never
have become Paul. So, too, if modern Sauls
knew what they were doing in persecuting the
Church, and knowing what they did, even with
the heavens rent and Christ's telling them they
were persecuting Him, they would be cast into
hell! It is not wisdom that saves—it is ignorance!

Every true follower of Christ knows he
must be hated by the world. "If the world hate
you, know you that it hath hated Me before
you. If you had been of the world, the world
would love its own: but because you are not of
the world, but I have chosen you out of the
world, therefore the world hateth you. Remember . . . the servant is not greater than his
Master." We must be hated even as Christ
Himself was hated. We must be abused as
Christ Himself was abused. We must be prepared to be told again and again that we are
ignorant because we do not know that modern
psychology has disproved a soul; that we are
benighted fools because we do not know that
higher Biblical criticism has destroyed the
authenticity of Scripture; that we are narrow-

minded because we do not accept the unmoral interpretations of God's laws; that we are a race of darkened minds because we do not know that evolution has proved original sin to be a myth; that we are ignorant because we do not know that science has dispensed with Providence, with God, and with Christ.

Yes, we are ignorant! ignorant of the false wisdom of the world; ignorant of the wisdom of the age; ignorant of all that false wisdom which would blind us to the lightening truths of the Eternal Sun; ignorant of modern pagan ways. Oh, Holy Father in Heaven, we thank Thee that we are ignorant—ignorant of those things which keep us from Thee! It is not the wisdom of the world that saves—it is ignorance!

Hence, there is not a loyal Catholic heart in the world, kneeling at the foot of the Cross, that is ignorant of the reason of all forgiveness, and from such a heart comes the plaintive prayer:

Oh, Jesus, I do not want to know the world; I do not want to know the pride of the world which crowns Thy head with thorns; I do not want to know how nails of selfishness are driven, nor how the spear of

220

bitterness is launched; I do not want to know how snowflakes are hammered, nor who turns about the Arcturus; I do not want to know the length of this great universe and its expanse in light-years; I do not want to know the breadth of the earth as it dances about the chariot of the sun; I do not want to know the heights of the stars as they glitter about the day's dead sanctities; I do not want to know the depth of the sea nor the secrets of its palace. I am willing to be ignorant of all these things. I want to know only one thing, and that is—the breadth and length and depth and height of Thy redeeming love on the Cross, Sweet Saviour of Men. I want, dear Jesus, to be ignorant of everything in this world—everything—but You! And then, by the strangest of strange paradoxes, I shall be wise!

TIME AND THE TIMELESS

IT IS not often nowadays that men speak of eternity; their thoughts are almost always on time. In fact, Time has become one of the most important things in the world. Some years ago, before physics became the fashionable science, the human mind was wont to conceive of time as something in which things happened. Now it is looked upon as the very fabric of the universe. Sacred Scripture tells us that a moment will come when there will be no more time. The unsacred scripture of our day tells us that Time is the very essence of things.

Would we seek for evidences of this mood of temporalism, we could find them in every nook and corner of the world to-day. In the field of morals, for example, the current doctrine is that any action is moral, provided the time in which we live regards it as moral. Religion, too, has drunk deep of the intoxicating draughts of temporalism, and now reeling under its effects, it preaches a religion wholly confined to Time, utterly oblivious of Eternity. It no longer asks a man to save his soul for Eternity; it asks him to save his body for Time. It is unconcerned about citizenship in the Kingdom of God, but tremendously excited about citizenship in the Kingdom of Time. That is, incidentally, why some modern religions stress birth-control, favoring as they do the economic motive that belongs to Time, rather than the religious motive which belongs to eternity. Philosophy, too, has become so obsessed with that notion that it teaches with unbuttoned pride that there is no such thing as Truth with a capital "T," for Truth is ambulatory: we make it as we go; it depends on the Time in which we live. There are not even wanting writers who have gone to the excess of saying that God is not in Eternity, but is in Time, or rather He is being produced by whole cosmic floods of Time, undergoing miraculous baptisms at the hands of Time, and being hurled onwards and forwards to some goal which is not yet certain, but which Time will reveal if we ever give it Time enough.

The Church is not in sympathy with this
226

mood of temporalism. It teaches that it is about time that we cease talking about Time, and begin to think of the Timeless. I therefore propose to prove the superiority of the Church's attitude over that of the modern world by showing first of all that Time stands in the way of real happiness, and secondly, that only in as much as we succeed in transcending Time do we ever begin to be happy.

Time is the one thing that makes real pleasure impossible, for the simple reason that it does not permit us to make a club-sandwich of pleasures. By its very nature, it forbids us to have many pleasures together under the penalty of having none of them at all. By the mere fact that I exist in Time, it is impossible for me to combine the pleasures of marching with the old guard of Napoleon, and at the same time, advancing under the flying eagles of Cæsar. By the mere fact that I live in Time, I cannot enjoy simultaneously the winter sports of the Alps, and the limpid waters of the Riviera. Time makes it impossible for me to be stirred by the oratory of a Demosthenes, and at the same time to listen to the melodious accents of the great Bossuet. Time does not permit me to combine the prudence that comes with age, and the buoyancy that belongs to youth. It is the one thing which prevents me from gathering around the same festive table with Aristotle, Socrates, Thomas Aquinas, and Mercier in order to learn the secrets of great minds in solving the riddles of a universe. If it were not for Time, Dante and Shakspere could have sipped tea together, and Homer even now might tell us his stories in English. It is all very nice and lovely to enjoy the mechanical perfections of this age of luxury, but there are moments when I would like to enjoy the calm and peace of the Middle Ages, but Time will not permit it. If I live in the twentieth century, I must sacrifice the pleasures of the thirteenth, and if I enjoy the Athenian age of Pericles, I must be denied the Florentine age of Dante.

Thus it is that Time makes it impossible to combine pleasures. I know there are advertisements which would invite us to dine and dance, but no one can do both comfortably at one and the same time. All things are good, and yet none can be enjoyed except in their season, and the enjoyment must always be tinged with

where the great pleasures of history would not
be denied us because of their historical in-
compatibility, but all unified in a beautiful
hierarchial order, like a pyramid in that all
would minister to the very unity of our personality. Suppose I say that I could reach a
point of Timelessness at which all the enjoy-
ments and beauties and happinesses of Time
could be reduced to those three fundamental
unities which constitute the perfection of our
being, namely, Life, and Truth, and Love, for
into these three all pleasures can be resolved.

Suppose first of all that I could reduce to a
single focal point all the pleasures of life, so
that in the "now" which never looked before
nor after, I could enjoy the life that seems to
be in the sea when its restless bosom is dimpled
with calm, as well as the urge of life that seems
to be in all the hill-encircling brooks that
loiter to the sea; the life which provokes the
dumb, dead sod to tell its thoughts in violets;
the life which pulsates through a springtime
blossom as the swinging cradle for the fruit;
the life of the flowers as they open the chalice
of their perfume to the sun; the life of the
birds as the great heralds of song and mes-

sengers of joy; the life of all the children that run shouting to their mothers' arms; the life of all the parents that beget a life like unto their own; and the life of the mind that on the wings of an invisible thought strikes out to the hid battlements of Eternity to the life whence all living comes. . . .

Suppose that in addition to concentrating all the life of the universe in a single point, I could also concentrate in another focal point all the truths of the world, so that I could know the truth the astronomer seeks as he looks up through his telescope, and the truth the biologist seeks as he looks down through his miscroscope; the truth about the heavens, and who shut up the sea with doors when it did burst forth as issuing from a womb; the truth about the hiding place of darkness and the treasure house of hail, and the cave of the winds; the truth about the common things: why fire, like a spirit, mounts to the heavens heavenly, and why gold, like clay, falls to the earth earthly; the truth the philosopher seeks as he tears apart with his mind the very wheels of the universe; the truth the theologian seeks as he uses Revelation to unravel the secrets of

God which far surpass those that John heard as he leaned his head upon the breast of his Master. . . .

Suppose that over and above all these pleasures of life and truth, there could be unified in another focal point all the delights and beauties of love that have contributed to the happiness of the universe: the love of the patriot for his country; the love of the soldier for his cause; the love of the scientist for his discovery; the love of the flowers as they smile upon the sun; the love of the earth at whose breast all creation drinks the milk of life; the love of mothers, who swing open the great portals of life that a child may see the light of day; the love of friend for friend to whom he could reveal his heart through words; the love of spouse for spouse; the love of husband for wife; and even the love of angel for angel, and the angel for God with a fire and heat sufficient to enkindle the hearts of ten thousand times ten thousand worlds. . . .

Suppose that all the pleasures of the world could be brought to these three focal points of life and truth and love, just as the rays of the sun are brought to unity in the sun; and sup-

233

pose that all the successive pleasures of Time could be enjoyed at one and the same "now"; and suppose that these points of unity on which our hearts and minds and souls would be directed, would not merely be three abstractions, but that the focal point in which all the pleasures of life were concentrated would be a life personal enough to be a Father, and that that focal point of truth in which all the pleasures of truth were concentrated, would not merely be an abstract truth, but a truth personal enough to be a Word or a Son, and that that focal point of love in which all the pleasures of love were concentrated, would be not merely an abstract love, but a love personal enough to be a Holy Spirit; and suppose that once elevated to that supreme height, happiness would be so freed from limitations that it would include these three as one, not in succession, but with a permanence; not as in Time, but as in the Timeless—then we would have Eternity, then we would have God! The Father, Son, and Holy Ghost: Perfect Life, Perfect Truth, Perfect Love. Then we would have happiness—and that would be heaven.

But will the pleasures of that Timelessness

with God and that enjoyment of life and truth
and love which is the Trinity be in any way
comparable to the pleasures of Time? Is there
anyone on this earth that will tell me about
heaven? Certainly there are three faculties to
which one might appeal, namely, to what one
has seen, to what one has heard, and to what
one can imagine. Will heaven surpass all the
pleasures of the eye, and the ear, and the imagination? First of all, will it be as beautiful
as some of the things that can be seen? I have
seen the Villa d'Este of Rome with its long
lanes of ilex and laurel, and its great avenues
of cypress-trees, all full of what might be called
the vivacity of quiet and living silence; I have
seen a sunset on the Mediterranean when two
clouds came down like pillars to form a brilliant red tabernacle for the sun and it glowing
like a golden host; I have seen, from the harbor, the towers and the minarets of Constantinople pierce through the mist which hung over
them like a silken veil; I have seen the château
country of France and her Gothic Cathedrals
aspiring heavenwards like prayers; I have
seen the beauties of the castles of the Rhine,
and the combination of all these visions al-

most makes me think of the door-keeper of the Temple of Diana who used to cry out to those who entered: "Take heed to your eye," and so I wonder if the things of Eternity will be as beautiful as the combined beauty of all the things which I have seen. . . .

I have not seen all the beauties of nature, others I have heard of that I have not seen: I have heard of the beauties of the hanging gardens of Babylon, of the pomp and dignity of the palaces of the Doges, of the brilliance and glitter of the Roman Forum as its foundations rocked with the tramp of Rome's resistless legions; I have heard of the splendor of the Temple of Jerusalem as it shone like a jewel in the morning sun; I have heard of the beauties of the garden of Paradise where four-fold rivers flowed through lands rich with the gold and onyx, a garden made beautiful as only God knows how to make a beautiful garden; I have heard of countless other beauties and joys of nature which tongue cannot describe, nor touch of brush convey, and I wonder if all the joys and pleasures of heaven will be as great as the combined beauty of all the things of which I have heard. . . .

Beyond what I have heard and seen, there are things which I can imagine: I can imagine a world in which there never would be pain, nor disease, nor death; I can imagine a world wherein every man would live in a castle, and in that commonwealth of castles there would be a due order of justice without complaint or anxiety; I can imagine a world in which the winter would never come, and in which the flowers would never fade, and the sun would never set; I can imagine a world in which there would always be a peace and a quiet without idleness, a profound knowledge of things without research, a constant enjoyment without satiety; I can imagine a world which would eliminate all the evils and diseases and worries of life, and combine all of its best joys and happiness, and I wonder if all the happiness of heaven would be like the happiness of earth which I can imagine. . . .

Will eternity be anything like what I have seen, or what I have heard, or what I can imagine? No, eternity will be nothing like anything I have seen, heard or imagined. Listen to the voice of God: "Eye hath not seen, nor ear heard, neither hath it entered into the

237

heart of man, what things God hath prepared for them that love Him."

If the Timeless so much surpasses Time that there can be found no parallel for it, then I begin to understand the great mystery of the shape of the human heart. The human heart is not shaped like a Valentine heart, perfect and regular in contour; it is slightly irregular in shape as if a small piece of it were missing out of its side. That missing part may very well symbolize a piece that a spear tore out of the universal heart of Humanity on the Cross, but it probably symbolizes something more. It may very well mean that when God created each human heart, He kept a small sample of it in heaven, and sent the rest of it into the world of Time where it would each day learn the lesson that it could never be really happy, never be really wholly in love, and never be really whole-hearted until it went back again to the Timeless to recover the sample which God had kept for it for all eternity.